Edna Lyall

Knight-Errant

Vol. 1

Edna Lyall

Knight-Errant
Vol. 1

ISBN/EAN: 9783743323230

Manufactured in Europe, USA, Canada, Australia, Japa

Cover: Foto ©ninafisch / pixelio.de

Manufactured and distributed by brebook publishing software (www.brebook.com)

Edna Lyall

Knight-Errant

KNIGHT-ERRANT.

VOL. I.

NEW AND POPULAR NOVELS

AT ALL THE LIBRARIES

A DATELESS BARGAIN. By C. L. PIRKIS, author of 'Lady Lovelace,' &c. 3 vols.

DRIVEN BEFORE THE STORM. By GERTRUDE FORDE, author of 'In the Old Palazzo,' &c. 3 vols.

COURTLEROY. By ANNE BEALE, author of 'Fay Arlington,' 'The Pennant Family,' &c. 3 vols.

VICTIMS. By THEO GIFT, author of 'Pretty Miss Bellew,' 'Visited on the Children,' 'Lil Lorimer,' &c. 3 vols.

PASSAGES IN THE LIFE OF A LADY, in 1814—1815—1816. By HAMILTON AIDE, author of 'Rita,' &c. 3 vols.

HURST & BLACKETT, 13, GREAT MARLBOROUGH STREET

KNIGHT-ERRANT

BY

EDNA LYALL

AUTHOR OF
'DONOVAN,' 'WE TWO,' 'IN THE GOLDEN DAYS,' ETC.

> But all through life I see a Cross,
> Where sons of God yield up their breath;
> There is no gain except by loss,
> There is no life except by death,
> There is no vision but by Faith,
> Nor glory but by bearing shame,
> Nor Justice but by taking blame;
> And that Eternal Passion saith,
> 'Be emptied of glory and right and name.'
> *Olrig Grange.* WALTER C. SMITH.

IN THREE VOLUMES.

VOL. I.

LONDON:
HURST AND BLACKETT, PUBLISHERS,
13, GREAT MARLBOROUGH STREET.
1887.

All rights reserved.

TO

EVANGELINE JAMESON.

'Searching my heart for all that touches you,
I find there only love and love's good-will.'

CONTENTS

OF

THE FIRST VOLUME.

Chap.		Page
I.	'THE HAPPIEST MAN IN NAPLES'	1
II.	A GOODLY HERITAGE	17
III.	FRANCESCA	36
IV.	A CLOUDLESS BETROTHAL	51
V.	A THREATENING SKY	76
VI.	THE STORM BREAKS	96
VII.	'NO ONE BUT YOU'	109
VIII.	PIALE SCHEMES	131
IX.	THE OLIVE GARDEN	155
X.	THE 'PILGRIM'	169
XI.	A FIRST ENCOUNTER	193
XII.	A TROUBLED NIGHT	222
XIII.	'PAZIENZA'	243
XIV.	THE NEW BARITONE	261
XV.	A DEAR ADVENTURE	283

KNIGHT-ERRANT.

CHAPTER I.

'THE HAPPIEST MAN IN NAPLES.'

'They came at a delicate plain called Ease, where they went with much content; but that plain was but narrow, so they were quickly got over it.'—*Pilgrim's Progress.*

'Presto! off with the paper! let us see how they look!' exclaimed a fresh, mellow voice.

'Permit me, signor,' interposed the Neapolitan stationer who presided behind the counter of a shop in the Toledo, and taking the little white packet from the hands of the speaker he slipped the blade of his penknife through the wrapper, drew forth with a flourish one of the cards within, and, bowing and smiling, handed it to his customer. 'There, signor, and accept with it my sincere congratulations.'

The young man glanced eagerly at the card, upon which was engraved in copperplate the name,—

'AVVOCATO CARLO POERIO DONATI.'

It was to him the sign and symbol of manhood, of freedom; it meant that he turned his back upon examinations and tutelage; it meant that he was at length free to declare the love which for many years had been the great guiding influence of his life.

'Ah, Signor Pietro,' he replied, turning to the friendly old shopkeeper with a smile which illumined his whole face; 'I am the happiest man in Naples to-day! Come, Enrico, you are not half enough excited!' and turning to his friend, who stood beside him watching the scene with good-humoured indifference, he caught a similar little packet from his hand, and, tearing it open, produced a card bearing the name,—

'AVVOCATO ENRICO RITTER.'

Enrico was of German parentage, but the

Ritters had lived for half-a-century in Naples and were naturalised; nevertheless, spite of his Italian education, Enrico remained German to the backbone, and presented in every way a most curious contrast to his friend and companion.

'Why, devil take the cards! they're not so much to me as to you,' he exclaimed, with a laugh. 'Signor Pietro does not expect to see me wild with excitement over a trumpery piece of pasteboard.'

'Most matter-of-fact Enrico! Where is your imagination?' cried Carlo, laughing. 'Can the magic word *Arrocato* call up to your German brain no visions of the future?'

'Visions!' grumbled Enrico, with assumed despondency; 'ay, visions of hot courts, long cases, rusty gowns, and scant fees.'

Both Carlo and the stationer laughed heartily at the dolorous face of the speaker.

'Well, Signor Pietro, it was ever the same story; was it not? He is prosaic now as when we came to you years ago for note-books and pens on our way from the *Ginnasio*. But come, it is getting late; I must be off, Enrico. Good-day to you, Signor Pietro, and many thanks for your congratulations.'

The two friends left the shop and walked on through the busy, crowded streets to the Piazza del Plebiscito. More than one passer-by turned to glance at Carlo's beautiful face; for, truth to tell, good looks are the exception, not the rule, in Naples, and among the swarthy or sallow Neapolitans his rich, ruddy-brown colouring could not fail to win notice. The face was singularly attractive, not only from the beauty of its well-cut features, but from the unaffected modesty of the expression and the sweetness of the dark, liquid eyes. He looked what he had termed himself—the happiest man in Naples. If in appearance he lacked anything it was height; but we cannot all be heroes of six feet, and Carlo, though small and slight, was so well proportioned, so lithe and active, so imbued with the grace common to most Italians, that it was impossible to wish for any change in him. He might that day have stood as a true impersonation of Optimism, while

Enrico Ritter, on the other hand, might well have posed as the ideal Pessimist.

Enrico was of the Germans, German; there was no mistaking that fair, straight hair and moustache, that light colouring and broad face, those small, light-grey eyes, honest, hard, yet with some good-humour in their expression which contradicted the cynical mouth. What had first drawn two such curiously contrasted men together it was impossible to say; scientists might have argued that it was the very fact that they were polar opposites. But, whatever the cause of their friendship, friends they were in the best sense of the word, and their friendship had stood the wear and tear of ten years.

By this time they had reached the Piazza; the afternoon sun was shining on the red walls of the Palazzo Reale, lighting up the heavy arcades of the San Carlo, glorifying the dome and stately front of the Church of S. Francesco di Paolo. It seemed a strange medley of ancient and modern, haunted by memories of King Bomba's cruelties,—haunted by visions of Garibaldi and Carlo Poerio, while hither and thither plied the busy tramcars, and amid a gay throng of people dressed in the latest Parisian fashion there filed slowly past a procession of white-robed monks.

'Ten minutes to spare before my horse is ready,' said Carlo, looking at his watch; 'let us have some coffee;' and so saying he led the way into the nearest restaurant. Enrico paused to buy an evening paper, then followed his friend.

The place was crowded, and there arose a confused babel of voices, a mingling of French, English, and Italian. Carlo had seated himself at one of the small marble tables, and, since Enrico seemed more inclined to read his paper than to talk, was fain to listen to the discussion going on between two English tourists close by.

Possibly they thought themselves practically alone in this foreign assembly; certainly it did not occur to them that their very Italian-looking neighbour understood and spoke their language as well as his own, for they were talking freely on subjects which Englishmen are not wont to speak of in public.

'But, really now,' urged the younger of the two, with some warmth, 'you can't possibly maintain such a notion. Do you think we are not improved,—vastly improved, in the last two hundred years?'

'The increase of civilisation gives us a better appearance, I grant,' said the elder, 'but I do not believe the sum total of evil is lessened.'

Carlo listened attentively, for this dreary doctrine was opposed to his whole nature.

'Why, turn to history,' exclaimed the younger man, 'see how indifferent people were to suffering, and then look at our nineteenth century, with its innumerable charities, its missions, its hospitals, its guilds.'

'True, quite true,' said the elder man, quietly; 'a wave of philanthropy is passing over us; there is much talk—even, I admit, much good work, but men are not more willing to live the life of the Crucified.'

The younger man was silent. Hitherto he had been very ready with his replies, now he fell into deep thought. Carlo Donati, too, was struck by those last words. They broke in very painfully upon his rapturous happiness, his joyful anticipations. He had been spared most of the usual doubts and fears of a lover; he was practically sure of Francesca Britton's love, and already he had received her father's permission to propose to her, Captain Britton having only stipulated that he should wait till his education was finished.

Now his time of probation was over; within a few days, nay, perhaps within a few hours, Francesca might be his own. Could he bear on that day, of all others, to dream of the possibility of a cloud arising? His sky was so clear, his life had been so happy and successful, the very thought of gathering darkness on the horizon was torture to him; 'Let my happiness last! oh, let it last!' was his inward cry, and, as if in answer, there floated back to him the stranger's words, and he knew that they were true: 'Men are not more willing to live the life of the Crucified.'

Involuntarily he turned to glance at the

man who had disturbed his peace, and saw a strong, intellectual face, which, notwithstanding traces of deep thought and hard conflict, bore a calm and tranquil expression. But the conversation had been checked by those grave words, the stranger called the waiter, paid for his coffee, tucked his 'Baedeker' under his arm, and rose to go.

Carlo followed him with his eyes as he left the restaurant; he felt strongly that curious conviction which comes to some people when a stranger has unconsciously influenced them, that in this world, or some other, they will infallibly meet again.

So engrossed had he been with the two Englishmen and their talk that he had not heeded his friend. He had not seen the start of surprise and dismay with which Enrico had noted a paragraph in the *Piccolo*. What was there in those brief lines which filled him with apprehension? Why did he glance with such anxiety and regret at Carlo, and then once again read that unwelcome paragraph?

'We understand that the season will be

commenced at Whitsuntide at the Teatro Mercadante, with the operatic company of Signor Merlino. Madame Merlino, whose singing has created a very favourable impression in America, will be the prima donna.'

All the indifference had vanished now from Enrico's face. A dreadful annoyance awaited his friend, and that it should reach him to-day of all days seemed to him intolerable. He would at any rate do his best to give him a respite, Carlo should at least propose to Miss Britton, and enjoy if it were even but a few hours of unalloyed happiness. Seizing his opportunity, when his companion turned to watch the Englishmen as they left the restaurant, Enrico tore off the corner containing the unwelcome news, and was about to thrust it into his pocket when Carlo checked him with a question,—

'What is it? About our examinations?'

'No,' said Enrico, composedly; 'I saw nothing about them. I only wanted a scrap of paper to wrap up these confounded cards; thanks to your eagerness to see them, they're all loose in my pocket.'

So saying, he deliberately wrapped the cards in the paper containing the bad news, and pushed the rest of the *Piccolo* towards his friend. 'Take it home with you if you like, I have done with it.'

'And I,' said Carlo, laughing, 'hope to have little time for it.' He took it nevertheless, stowed it away in his pocket and got up to go.

'I'll walk with you as far as the stable,' said Enrico. 'Now follow my advice and ride home calmly. If you go on in this state of fever you will not be fit for your interview with that stately old Englishman, upon whom you have to make a good impression as future son-in-law.'

'Stuff and nonsense!' said Carlo, laughing gaily. 'Make an impression, indeed! Do you forget that we have been next-door neighbours this age, and that he knows me as well as you do?'

'An impossibility,' said Enrico, smiling, 'for with me I have taught you, as we say in Germany, to be as you are to yourself. Now with that old English captain you walk as though treading on eggs, you are courteous and deferential; you never forget that you hope to be his son-in-law, and you'll never quarrel with him,— at any rate not until the hope has become a tame reality.'

The dry, sardonic tone in which this had been spoken, turned Carlo's indignant protest to laughter.

'The only topic on which we are likely to quarrel is politics; and as he knows nothing of Italian affairs, one needs now and then adroitly to turn the conversation. But don't make me speak against Captain Britton, to-day, *amico mio*.'

'Ah, poor fellow!' said Enrico, pityingly; 'I knew he would prove the crumpled rose-leaf to destroy your perfect bliss. There is always a father-in-law, or a mother-in-law, or a cantankerous relative, who kicks up a row about the settlements. Don't you expect the course of your true love to run smooth — that's against nature.'

As he spoke he glanced rather anxiously at a large hoarding which they were approaching, rapidly running his eye over the theatrical posters, but, much to his relief, the Mercadanto bills were not yet out.

'You are as depressing as a funeral!' said Carlo, much tickled by the notion that the substantial Englishman was a crumpled rose-leaf; 'and, indeed, if I have no worse crook in my lot than Captain Britton, I shall fare well. No one could have been more courteous and helpful to my mother all these years, no one could have been more genial and hospitable to me. Of course we all have our faults.'

'Too true!' said Enrico, mockingly. 'The Englishman loves a lord, and has an eye to the main chance, and knows that you are heir to a certain rich uncle, and that unless the money is secured and tied up in the orthodox English fashion, it will all be flung away upon "Young Italy," or some hare-brained scheme for educating organ-grinders.'

'If we were not in the public street I would punish you well!' cried Carlo. 'There never was such a fellow for imputing low motives to all the world.'

'Well, well, rail at me as you like,' said

Enrico, indifferently; 'but as yet I have never found myself at fault in assuming that egoism rules the universe. Ah, your horse is waiting for you, I see, and the ostler tries to look hot and tired to cajole a large coin from you. *A rivederci!* But I advise you to avoid Naples for the next few days; don't come to me for sympathy in your rapture, for I've not the smallest doubt that love is egoism, and marriage is egoism, and ——'

'You are incorrigible!' cried Carlo, as he mounted the beautiful Arab which was waiting for him. 'I'll not wait to hear you out.' And, with a wave of the hand, he rode off, looking back laughingly at the interrupted egoist, who, with a shrug of the shoulders, turned away.

And yet it was something quite other than egoism which brought a grave look to Enrico's face as he walked home through the sunny streets. Suddenly perceiving an upright, alert-looking old man on the opposite side of the way, he crossed the road and hastened after him.

'Pardon me, Signor Piale!' he exclaimed, 'but may I ask you a question? You are probably acquainted with all that is going on in the musical world. Is this true that I see to-day in the *Piccolo?* Is Merlino's Company really coming to the Mercadante?'

'*Diavolo!* it is true enough, more's the pity,' replied the old man; 'but I have not said a word of it to my pupil. Carlo is over-sensitive, he felt that affair too much; only of late has he seemed to have forgotten it somewhat. He is one whose life should have been exempt from shadows.'

'I should have thought common decency would have kept Merlino away from Naples,' said Enrico, hotly.

'Merlino does not care a fig for common decency,' said the old musician. 'He is no credit to our profession. Probably he knows well enough that the Merlino-Donati scandal is just fresh enough in men's minds to make his operas draw well.'

'Let us, at least, do our best to keep back the ill news as long as possible,' said Enrico; 'it will be a frightful annoyance to Carlo just now, and I do believe it will be the death of his mother.'

''Tis always the innocent who suffer for the

guilty,' said the old singing-master, giving a fierce rub to his parchment-like cheek. 'If ever there was one who deserved to be free from care, why it is Carlo; there are but few now-a-days who could show so blameless a life.'

'You speak very truly,' said Enrico. 'Let us hope his blameless life will weigh with worthy Captain Britton, and prove heavier than the family skeleton.'

CHAPTER II.

A GOODLY HERITAGE.

' It is not best in an inglorious ease
To sink and dull content,
When wild revolts and hopeless miseries
The unquiet nations fill ;

 . . . . .

Nay, best it is indeed
To spend ourselves upon the general good;
And, oft misunderstood,
To strive to lift the knees and limbs that bleed.
This is the best, the fullest meed.
Let ignorance assail or hatred sneer
Who loves his race he shall not fear ;
He suffers not for long,
Who doth his soul possess in loving, and grows strong.'
LEWIS MORRIS.

THE old singing-master had not exaggerated matters. Though inclined to see everything connected with his favourite pupil through rose-coloured spectacles, his words were in this instance strictly true. Carlo had passed scathless through all the temptations of Neapolitan life; his history would bear the full light of day; it was impossible to imagine any one more strictly honourable, more simple and open-minded. But then, certainly, Nature had been to him almost prodigal in her gifts. To begin with, he came of a good family, and that not in the vulgar acceptation of the word. The Donati were not of noble birth, but for five or six generations they had been well educated, and had earned quite an unusual reputation in the various learned professions which they had followed. Faults of temper or of judgment they might have shown, but no Donati had ever been guilty of an act of meanness, nor had there been in any one of them a single grain of insincerity. To belong to a family which has earned well-deserved respect, to be able to look back upon forefathers who have lived well and bravely, to know that before you existed your father, and his father before him, spoke for freedom and pleaded the cause of the people, this is indeed a birthright worth having. An inheritance of money may or may not be a desirable thing, but an inheritance of character, an ancestry of generous, true-hearted men, who did justly, and loved mercy, and walked humbly with their God, this is a thing that kings might covet.

Carlo had undoubtedly inherited a noble character, or rather had inherited certain tendencies, and as yet, by his life, had helped to develope, not to arrest, their growth.

At the close of the last century there had been born a certain Bruno Donati. People had prophesied great things of him; he had established, with almost unheard-of rapidity, a great reputation as an advocate, he had married a beautiful heiress, he was assuredly a man who would 'rise'—so said the world. He did rise, but not in the way predicted. Regardless of his reputation, regardless of self altogether, he joined the patriot party who were struggling to overthrow the hated tyranny of the Neapolitan Bourbons. Leaving his home, and taking a tender farewell of his wife and his little children, he set off one June morning for Cilento, the place which had been chosen for a small rising. At first a certain measure of success encouraged the patriots; they were able to take the little fort of Palinuro, and to hoist the tricoloured flag.

But those brave pioneers knew well that they were taking their lives in their hands. They had achieved a success which must draw the attention of the whole country upon them. In hot haste General Delcaretto was sent down to attack them with six thousand men, and no mercy was shown. Twenty of the patriots were shot without trial; twenty-six others, and amongst them Bruno Donati, were executed. The young advocate had, as it seemed, sacrificed his life for a hopeless cause; he was never again to return to his beautiful home, but General Delcaretto caused his head to be paraded in front of the house before the eyes of his widow and his fatherless children. Then, when the people had been ruined, a commune or two suppressed, and the insurrection completely stamped out, the General returned to Naples to be rewarded for his gallantry by receiving the title of Marquis, a decoration of a knightly order, and a pension.

Bruno Donati's widow did not die until she had educated her two sons, and had seen that the younger one, also Bruno, was likely to be just such a man as his father. She did not realise how much alike the story of the two Brunos would be.

Both sons followed their father's profession, but the younger one was so much engrossed in the revolutionary movement of the time that he did not make much way in it. Instead of so doing, he joined 'Young Italy,' studied deeply under the guidance of Mazzini, and at length enrolled himself in Garibaldi's gallant little army.

Carlo's earliest recollections were of a hot August day in the year 1862. He, as a little fellow, had sat beside his mother in a carriage outside the post-office at Pozzuoli, and some one had brought them the news of Garibaldi's defeat at Aspromonte, and with that the tidings that Bruno Donati was dangerously wounded. Carlo could even now see vividly his mother's deathly face as she read the news, could remember his puzzled wonder as to what it all meant, and whether it could possibly be that his father would never return.

But the second Bruno Donati was in some ways happier than his father; he was brought back from Aspromonte to his own home, where he lingered for a month—a month which proved of extraordinary value in his son's education. The child was too young to feel his father's death as a life-long grief, but he was just old enough to carry away from that death-bed a beautiful and unfading memory. Upon his childish brain was stamped the conviction that to die for '*La Patria*' was a very happy thing, that the sacrifice of self for others was the only true greatness, and that even such a failure as Aspromonte was not to be accounted failure—that right could not fail in the long run. '*Pazienza! pazienza!*' was the word constantly on the lips of the dying patriot—the word which always connected itself with his memory in the mind of his son. On Bruno Donati's dying face there had been that 'look of faith in renunciation' which was stamped upon the face of his teacher, Mazzini, and the look lived on in the child's heart.

'Carlino,' his father had said tenderly, on the very last day of his life,—'Carlino *mio*, thou wilt be a man one day.'

'How nice it will be when I am a man like you, father!' cried the boy eagerly.

The dying man smiled sadly.

'Remember always to comfort and shield thy mother; and Nita—take good care of Nita.'

'Why, father, Nita is older than I am, a whole year older!' exclaimed the child.

'But Nita is a woman, and my Carlo must be her brave protector; promise me that, my son.'

'I promise, father,' said the little fellow, squeezing the cold hand that clasped his. 'And father, dear father, I may have your sword, may I not? You'll not leave it to Uncle Guido, who has one already? For if I have it, father, then I could fight the brigands if they took Nita; could I not?'

The dying man smiled, touched by the innocent literalness of the reply. He caught Carlo to his breast, holding him in a long, close embrace.

'Why, father, I do believe you'll soon be well!' cried the boy, gleefully, feeling the power of those strong arms round him. He did not know that a sudden strength is often death's forerunner.

And in a sense he little meant his words came true, for by the next morning the second Bruno Donati had entered into the martyr's rest, and it was 'well' with him.

After this Carlo's life had been uneventful; the recollection of his father did not sadden him, on the contrary, it raised and stimulated him. For an Italian boy he had an unusually free and healthy life; his mother could never make up her mind to leave the country-house where they had been passing their *villeggiatura* during that summer of 1862, and in which her husband had died. They lived all the year round at the Villa Bruno, and a kindly old priest at Pozzuoli taught the boy until he was old enough to go in every day to the *Ginnasio* at Naples.

Here he entered into his lifelong friendship with Enrico Ritter, and learnt much through his intercourse with the German family, whose house became his head-quarters when he was in Naples. The Ritters, deeming the country life dull for the boy, were constantly inviting him to stay with them, and giving him brief snatches of gaiety. Nominally Lutherans, the worthy Germans were practically materialists, and it was largely owing to his visits at the Ritters that Carlo first became dissatisfied with the religion in which his mother had educated him. Equally was he dissatisfied with the conventional acceptance of Christianity and the real scepticism which prevailed in the Ritter household. For a year or two he puzzled his brain over the vexed question; finally he took the decisive step and resolved to go no more to church. This caused much pain to his mother and to his old friend, Father Cristoforo; and though plunging deeply into that sort of worship at the shrine of beautiful Nature which is the reaction from formalism, he felt a want in his life.

Shortly before this a house close to the Villa Bruno, which for some years had been untenanted, had been taken by an Englishman named Captain Britton. He had just lost his wife; and the home at San Remo, where his children had been born, and to which he had returned year by year when off duty, had grown intolerable to him. He retired from the service, and, taking a fancy to the neighbourhood of

Naples, settled down at Casa Bella, and made up his mind to live and die there. He had only two children—Francesca, a beautiful girl about a year younger than Carlo—so named after an Italian friend of the family—and Sibyl, a fairy-like little child of two years old. Miss Claremont, Francesca's governess, or, as everyone called her, 'Clare,' had the management of the house, and it was largely owing to her that a very close intimacy soon sprang up between the two neighbouring families.

Carlo and Francesca were at first not of an age for falling in love. They became fast friends, and Carlo in his rather lonely life was enchanted to find that the English girl was allowed almost unlimited freedom. She was wholly unlike his convent-bred sister, who, since her mother was an invalid, was allowed to come home now and then for a day or two. Nita was beautiful, and sang like an angel, and was a devout little Catholic, and did her best to teach him the error of his ways. But, to save her life, Nita could not have been a companion in his games. Now Francesca, though no hoyden, was in the matter of games as good as a boy. She was not above climbing trees or running races, she excelled at rounders, she even initiated him into the mysteries of cricket, enlisting the services of Clare and the gardeners.

Then nothing would do but he must teach her to row, and many were the happy hours they spent on the sea together, sometimes with Clare in the stern, sometimes with little Sibyl and her nurse, sometimes with old Florestano, the fisherman, who would tell them quaint legends of saints, or mermaids, or ghosts, in all of which he believed equally. Sometimes they would go oyster-catching in Lake Fusaro, or, with Clare as a delightful third, would scramble about in the Acropolis at Cumæ, seeking to make fresh discoveries. Or they would play hide-and-seek in the Grotto della Pace, or act thrilling brigand stories, or dig and search in field or vineyard, and perhaps stumble across the remains of an old Roman villa or the ruins of a temple, hidden away by the straggling green growth.

Those were happy days for all of them. Carlo before long formed for Miss Claremont that sort of reverential, half-worshipping friendship and admiration which is not uncommon between boys of his age and middle-aged women. And Clare was a friend worth having. She influenced people chiefly by loving them; you never felt with her that she was trying to doctor you, or to improve your moral or spiritual health. She discussed many things with Carlo, listened to his crude, half-fledged ideas with the utmost patience, and would no more have smiled at them or treated them contemptuously than a woman would smile with contempt as she watches the staggering steps of a baby beginning to walk alone.

Clare sympathised much with the difficulties of his position; she saw that his deeply religious Italian nature would never rest content in its present isolation.

'Do you never feel the need of worshipping?' she asked him one day.

'Yes,' he replied, 'but one need not be within the walls of a church to do that; a boat at sea, or an olive-grove, are more to my taste.'

Just at that time he was the least bit proud

of having shaken himself free from the bondage of Romanism, a fact which was quite patent to Clare, and proved to her how perilous was his state.

'And yet,' she urged, 'I should have thought that you—a follower of Mazzini—would have had a strong faith in Association.'

The words struck home, unpleasantly convincing Carlo that he had been rapturously hugging a thing which he called Freedom, and that it was but an illusion more worthy to be called Isolation.

'I don't know where to turn to!' he exclaimed, chafed by a remark which had disturbed his peace, and proved it to be false.

'Are you trying to find out the best place?' she asked quietly.

He was silent, and Clare, who had the rare tact to know when she had said enough, changed the subject.

But the very next Sunday he astonished her by asking leave to join their party and drive in to the English church at Naples with them. His total absence of false shame, and the ingenuous humility which could thus tacitly own itself in the wrong, promptly and publicly following the suggestion of a woman, were thoroughly Italian. Clare reflected that an Englishman would have allowed a week or two to pass by, in order to prove that he came of his own free will and not at the instigation of another; or would, perhaps, have toiled over on foot in the early morning, slinking in at the back of the church, in terror lest people should comment on the amendment of his ways.

After a time he formally joined the English Church. Of course he had some opposition to encounter; but though his old friend the priest shook his head sorrowfully, and though his mother shed tears, and though the Ritters chaffed him good-humouredly, his happiness was too great to be marred by such things; besides they all loved him so well that they soon pardoned the obnoxious step which he had taken, and did their best to forget that he was not as they were.

A few months after this the first shadow fell upon Carlo's perfect felicity. It was suddenly arranged that the Britton household should migrate to England for a year. An aunt of Francesca's had just died, and some one was urgently needed to look after the motherless children. Who so fit for such a task as Clare? and though she would fain have lived on in that happy Italian home, she could not linger there when needed in another place, and at any rate she should have her children for yet another year. That helped to break the parting. Captain Britton was glad for a time to be with his brother, and a year of English life, in which to finish Francesca's rather unconventional education, was deemed a good idea by all. So once more Casa Bella was silent and deserted, and Carlo was left to his own devices.

It was just at this time that Nita returned from her convent. A great change was at once effected in the peacefulness of the Villa Bruno, for the girl, while retaining enough of her religious education to make her persecute her heretic brother with endless arguments and remonstrances, was yet so wearied of its strict restraint that she broke out into violent reaction and tyrannised over her mother, much as she herself had till now been tyrannised over.

The Signora Donati was an invalid; she had never recovered from the cruel shock of her husband's death, nor had she at any time been noted for strength of character. Carlo had been too loyal ever to take advantage of this; her slightest wish had been to him a command, and the two had idolised each other. But somehow it happened that Nita coming home from her convent felt like an intruder; she could not find a niche for herself in the home, and, measuring the hearts of other people by her own, fancied she was not cared for. Perhaps her mother did show a little too markedly that Carlo was her favourite; but then it really was difficult not to love the son who treated her with such tenderness, such respectful devotion, somewhat better than the daughter, who sought for nothing but her own amusement, and never voluntarily performed for her the slightest service.

It was also, perhaps, true that Carlo did not greatly care for his sister, at any rate she tried his temper severely. He was impatient with her aggravating little displays of piety, her deep genuflexions, her paraded fasts. He was constantly detecting her in petty deceits, and once, after some worse specimen of duplicity than usual, he had angrily upbraided her.

'You are not fit to bear the name of Donati,' he cried hotly, his boyish sense of honour deeply wounded, and his family pride hurt to find that Nita was no better than the rest of the world.

'Perhaps I shall not bear it much longer!' she retorted angrily.

And those words haunted poor Carlo for many a year. For, not long after, all Naples rang with the news that Anita Donati had eloped with her singing-master, a certain *basso* who had been engaged that winter at the San Carlo.

Fortunately the Villa Bruno was far away in the country, and the Signora too great an invalid to go into society. She could bear her agony in solitude, and was not obliged to wear a mask and go about as though nothing had happened.

But Carlo was in the thick of the fray, he had to listen to Uncle Guido's indignant denunciations, he had to bear the brunt of the endless questions of the outsiders, had to endure the bitter consciousness that his sister's name was being bandied about in the city, and that, for the first time, a Donati had incurred well-merited blame.

Since then nothing had been heard of Anita, except that about a week after her flight she had forwarded to her mother a newspaper with the announcement of her marriage. But the Signora Donati never recovered from the shock, nor could she ever forgive herself, for she rightly felt that had her relations with her daughter been happier such a thing could never have happened.

Five years had gone by since then, and Time had passed his quieting hand over both grief and disgrace. Certainly Carlo felt nothing but happiness—unalloyed happiness—as he rode home from Naples that sunny spring day. He knew nothing of that ominous little paragraph torn out of the *Piccolo*, but galloped on over the white, dusty road, past fields of Indian corn, past olive-gardens and vineyards, through the long, dark grotto of Posilipo, and on towards the picturesque little southern town of Pozzuoli. He scarcely noticed all the beauty round him; he could see nothing but the face of his dreams; and the very horse-hoofs flying over the road seemed to repeat again and again the word, 'Francesca! Francesca! Francesca!'

CHAPTER III.

FRANCESCA.

'Mortal! if life smile on thee, and thou find
   All to thy mind,
Think, Who did once from Heaven to Hell descend
   Thee to befriend;
So shalt thou dare forego, at His dear call,
   Thy best, thine all.'—KEBLE.

WHILE Carlo rode back from Naples, and while Signor Merlino and his operatic company steamed between the Pillars of Hercules into the blue Mediterranean, Francesca Britton sat in a little stone belvedere in the garden of Casa Bella, from time to time raising her eyes from her needle-work to glance at that same blue Mediterranean, or at the lovely mountains in Ischia, which were plainly visible through the arched doorway.

Beautiful as a child, Francesca was more than beautiful in early womanhood—she was lovely. It was not alone that the outline of cheeks and chin was perfect, that the nose was finely chiselled, that the masses of dark hair drawn back from the white forehead were rich and wavy; all this might be set down in black and white without conveying the faintest idea of what she was. And in truth this had happened over and over again; the photographers had done what they could, but had failed grievously. Photography could not give the ineffable charm of her ever-varying expression, the depth and sweetness of her dark-grey eyes, the dimple in her cheek, which seemed indeed the sign and symbol of her sunshiny nature. It could not convey the least notion of her shy grace, of her delicate purity, or of that keen sense of humour which sparkled so deliciously in her home-life. Outsiders sometimes deemed the beautiful English girl cold and distant, and a country life had tended to increase her natural shyness; but even had she lived in the midst of the fashionable world, Francesca Britton never could have been thoroughly known out of her own circle,—she was one of those who keep their best for their own.

She was roused from a reverie by seeing

a little miniature of herself flying down the straight, sunny walk which led to the summer-house, bordered on either side by azaleas glowing with crimson blossom, and tall, white oleanders.

'Dino sent me,' panted the little girl,—'Dino sent me with this for father. Where is father? They thought he was out here. And only fancy! Dino says, Fran dear, that Carlo came and rang the bell just like a visitor, and handed in his card. Think of Carlo ringing the bell!'

And Sibyl broke into a peal of laughter as she skipped about the summer-house. Her sister let her needlework fall, and taking the card, glanced at it, smiling and blushing in a way that would have enraptured anyone but unobservant Sibyl.

'Dino, he is nodding, and smiling, and looking so funny!' continued the little girl; 'and he says Carlo has perhaps come a-courting, but he won't tell me what it means. What is courting, Fran? Anything to do with the new tennis-court?'

''Tis a game which you play for love, Sibyl

dear. There, run and take the card to father, he is down in the orange-grove.'

The little messenger flew off again on her errand, and Francesca sat musing, smiling to herself every now and then as she thought of the beloved name with its novel prefix. Carlo an 'Avvocato;' it was too funny! And how like him to send in his card and be shown into the drawing-room so ceremoniously, instead of, as usual, just leaping over the hedge of prickly pear which divided the gardens of Casa Bella and Villa Bruno. Then delicious tremours, that were neither hope nor fear, ran through her, and her heart beat fast and loud. She could bear the stillness no longer, and, rising, she left the summer-house and walked down the path between the oleanders and the azaleas. All at once quick footsteps fell upon her ear; then, through the trees, she caught sight of the lithe, graceful figure so familiar to her. Ah! how foolish she was. Had they not been the best of friends for years and years? Why could she not go and meet him naturally to-day? Scolding herself roundly, she stopped because her feet refused to advance another step, and, with fingers which trembled visibly, tried to break off a spray of the crimson flowers.

'It is too stiff for you!' exclaimed Carlo, turning the corner and hurrying towards her.

'No, no!' she protested, laughing; 'you always misdoubt my powers;' and putting force upon her unruly fingers she broke off the spray. 'Here is a buttonhole for the "Avvocato," with his friend's congratulations.'

'The "Avvocato" is not content, he craves something more,' said Carlo, smiling.

'Very well; old playmates must not stand on ceremony,' she said gaily, well pleased that she had regained her self-possession; 'come to the belvedere, and I will put some maidenhair with it.'

They walked together up the path, Francesca pausing to pluck two or three pieces from a jungle of maidenhair growing about the old stones.

'There!' she exclaimed as they sat down in the cool little arbour while she twisted the ferns among the flowers; 'now are you content?'

'Not quite,' he said; 'I am clumsy, you will put them in for me.'

She fastened the flowers in his coat, and again her tiresome fingers began to tremble. Carlo, blessing the sight, snatched her hand in his and kissed it passionately.

'Francesca, forgive me!' he cried, 'I could wait no longer; you will not grudge me that one kiss. My darling, my darling, I have waited such years for you!'

His face, glowing with love, and devotion, and eager hope, was raised to hers. She only saw it for a moment, for something made a mist rise before her eyes, and when she could see clearly again she did not dare to meet his gaze; she looked instead out at the blue Mediterranean.

'I have loved you, Francesca, since you came back from England,—since you came and brought light and happiness to us after that dark time. I told your father,—begged him to let me speak to you, and he bade me wait. I have waited nearly five years, Francesca, and, oh! at times I scarcely knew how to trust myself here. Again and again I almost broke my word; but now your father gives me leave to come to you, to confess my love. My darling, look at me,—speak to me!'

She turned and gazed right into his eager, wistful eyes, a long, sweet, steadfast look; then her lips began to quiver a little, but thought better of it and smiled instead.

'What do you want me to say?'

'Say,' he cried eagerly, 'say, "I will try to love you."'

She shook her head.

'I can never say that,' she replied, and once more looked out seawards.

But the vehemence, the fire of his Italian nature, half frightened her. Despair was written on his face, despair rang in his voice, he did not pause one moment to reflect.

'Francesca! Francesca!' he cried, 'don't tell me I have come too late. My love! my love! I can't live without you. Unsay that "never."'

Grieved beyond measure that words so playfully meant should have called forth such a tropical outburst, she wreathed her arms about his neck, and pressed her face to his.

'Carlo *mio*,' she sobbed, 'don't break my heart

by misunderstanding me, I can never try to love you—because—because—I love you already.'

The depth of love and tenderness in her voice, the sweet abandonment of her manner—more really maidenly in its perfect sincerity than any coyness or hesitation—all this heightened to bliss Carlo's rapture of love. The momentary mistake, the cloud-shadow that had threatened his sky, made the sunshine all the more exquisite. He could not speak a word, but only clasped her close in the long sweet embrace which symbolised their betrothal.

'My own!' he murmured at last. 'My own, you gave me one terrible minute. To be without you, Francesca, that would be to be crucified!'

He did not definitely think of the talk between the two Englishmen, but the thought suggested that afternoon had sunk deep into his mind, and the agony of the brief mistake gave the emphatic utterance of that last word a tenfold power. Francesca breathed fast; Love unfolded to her his wonderful face, hitherto veiled; she was awed by the thought of the immortal passion, the undying devotion of her lover. The strength and sacredness of that last word he had used, filled her heart with a wondering love and humility. His happiness, his life, was in her keeping. And hers in his. Mortal man could never bear the strain of the one thought without the support of the other.

After a while they began to weave golden visions of the future; Carlo suggesting one place and another, for which he thought she had a fancy; a certain ideal nook, called Quisisana, on the other side of Naples, where once, years before, she had said she would like to build a house if someone would but leave her a fortune; a pretty villa at Posilipo, which she used to admire. It touched her to see how he remembered all her careless, girlish speeches, and had treasured them up for years.

'Ah,' she said, smiling, 'I used to think place would make such a difference; but now, Carlo *mio*, I don't care one bit. We will make a home in the wilderness, if it so pleases you, or at Naples, in a corner of an old palace—'tis all one to me so long as we are together.'

He drew her yet closer to him. They went

on weaving their plans unconscious of a small sprite approaching the summer-house. Sibyl stood composedly in the doorway for a moment, quite unnoticed by the lovers.

'Oh!' she ejaculated at length, 'is that the game?'

Her perplexed and rather disappointed look was most comical.

'What game?' asked Francesca, laughing and blushing.

'The game you said people played for love!'

'Yes, this is it,' said Carlo, laughing immoderately.

'Is that all?' exclaimed the sprite, in a tone of deep disappointment.

They only laughed.

'Well, for my part,' said Sibyl, who had caught many old-fashioned little phrases from living always with grown-up people, 'for my part, I think it's very dull.'

She ran off. Carlo watched her out of sight, smiling at her quaint disapproval.

'She will miss you, poor little one,' he said at last.

'Yes, that would be one reason for not going far away. And your mother, Carlo! How selfish of me not to remember her! You must never be parted from her—never.'

'You will be to her in the place of Nita,' said Carlo. 'You will comfort her as I have never been able to do.'

And so once again they plunged into the golden glories of the future. Clare must be persuaded to come back again, and take Sibyl in charge, and their paradise should be the Villa Bruno, already dear to them through many associations. That plan would obviate all difficulties, and render partings unnecessary; would be the happiest plan for others as well as for themselves.

'And we must not be selfish in our happiness,' said Francesca.

'No,' he replied, smiling as he remembered his friend's parting words, 'we will prove to Enrico Ritter that love is not selfishness, and that egoism does not rule the world, as he thinks.'

A gong sounding within the house warned

Carlo that he ought to go. Together they left the little stone summer-house and wandered through the lovely garden,—a garden wholly un-English. The scorching sun would not admit of lawns, but nevertheless there was a great charm in the straight, shady walks, with here and there an umbrella-pine, or a tall and sombre cypress mingling with limes, chestnuts, and camphor-trees. A long colonnade of white pillars was festooned from end to end with honeysuckle; vines linked together the bushy mulberry-trees; Indian corn grew green and ribbon-like beneath; while about all was that delicious sweetness only to be met with in the gardens of Italy. The house was solid and unpretentious, its whiteness relieved by masses of the feathery green pepper-tree, and a glory of climbing red geranium. Captain Britton sat in the loggia, which was wreathed with white roses. He looked up smiling as he saw the two drawing near, then came forward to bestow a kiss upon his daughter and a hearty hand-shake upon his future son-in-law. He was a large-limbed, strong-looking man, somewhat heavily built, with scanty grey hair and whiskers, and a broad smiling mouth. In manner he was kindly, genial, and patronising. But, spite of some surface faults, he was a thoroughly good-hearted man, and there was no mistaking his genuine hospitality and anxiety to help his friends. If Carlo occasionally winced beneath his benign patronage, or was provoked to anger by some show of insular prejudice, such trifles were soon forgotten in the recollection of the thousand acts of kindness shown both to his mother and to himself by the neighbourly Englishman. And then the Donati were proverbially susceptible, and Carlo had long been on his guard, and had schooled himself into thinking that the small discords and jarring notes which now and then occurred in the intercourse with the Brittons were really owing to his own ultra-sensitiveness. Such things were, after all, but trifles light as air, and were powerless really to disturb the bliss of being near his love.

'Hearty congratulations,' said the old Captain, warmly. 'I had not much fear that my little Fran would be unkind to you, and I suppose I must not grumble at losing her. I little thought that some day she would be changing into a Signora. But, there, we have made half an Englishman of you already; have we not?'

'No, no,' said Francesca, quick to note that the last words brought a momentary gleam of anger into her lover's eyes. 'Carlo will always be true to his country, though he speaks English almost like a native. That is because I taught you, Carlo *mio*; is it not?'

'Without love of the teacher learning is drudgery,' said Carlo, laughing. 'I enjoyed my English lessons.'

'That reminds me of your old master, Signor Piale. Oh, what will he say to us, Carlo? What will he say?' and Francesca laughed merrily.

'My kind regards to Signora Donati,' said Captain Britton, smiling. 'And if I may be permitted to call and pay my respects ——'

'To-night,' interrupted Carlo, eagerly. 'Say you will come to-night, after dinner. My mother cannot leave the house, you know, and she will be longing to see Francesca.'

'Well, well, no need to stand on ceremony even

to-day; we are such old friends, are we not?' said the Captain, good-naturedly. 'After dinner, then—after dinner. Come, Fran, my dear, no need to see Carlo off the premises, you'll meet again before long, and the soup is getting cold.'

Francesca was borne off to the dining-room, and Carlo, turning away, cleared the prickly pears at a bound, and alighted amid a group of lemon-trees in his own garden.

CHAPTER IV.

A CLOUDLESS BETROTHAL.

> 'Let my voice be heard that asketh
> Not for fame and not for glory;
> Give for all our life's dear story,
> Give us Love and give us Peace!'
>
> JEAN INGELOW.

VILLA BRUNO was a smaller house than Casa Bella. It was lacking, too, in the air of cosy English comfort which the Brittons had managed to impart to their rooms, and the furniture was scanty, though handsome of its kind. Carlo walked through the verandah and entered by the open window of the *salotto*, treading lightly, as he saw that his mother lay asleep on her couch. He stole up to her, and stood in silence, watching the beautiful but worn face of the invalid. He thought how great a happiness was in store for her, and smiled. He imagined Francesca bringing that English air of home into this room, and thought how sweet it would be when he rode home each evening to picture those two together waiting for him. Looking on into the sunny future, he forgot the present; his mother had opened her eyes, and had watched him for some moments before he saw that she was awake.

At last he looked down at her, and met her eyes shining into his with perfect comprehension.

'Carlino, you bring me good news!' she exclaimed, drawing his face down to hers, and kissing the smooth, ruddy-brown cheek.

'The best news, mother—the best!' he replied, returning her embrace. 'Oh, mother! I'm the happiest man in Italy.'

'Francesca ——' began the Signora.

'Francesca is mine—is mine!' he broke in. 'She is coming—you will see her soon, *madre mia.*'

'And her father?'

'Was kindness itself. He will bring her in this evening to see you. No one could have been more friendly. I saw him first, and then—then he told me I might speak to her—that I should find her in the garden. Afterwards, her first thought was for you. Oh, mother, she will be to you the daughter you have so much needed.'

The tears started to the mother's eyes.

'*Insomma!* Now I have grieved you, and made you think of poor Nita; happiness made me forget all else. Forgive me, little mother; I did not mean to make you think of the past.'

'Ah!' sobbed the Signora Donati. 'How can I help thinking of it, Carlino, when the contrast is so sharp—you coming to me thus with your joy as a son should, and Nita bringing me only shame and grief and disgrace—not even sending me one line of love or regret all these years?'

'She will come back, little mother,—she will come back,' he said, soothingly. 'Some day she will feel her need of you. Don't cry to-night, of all nights in the year. I shall take it as a bad omen.'

Years had raised no barrier between these two; Carlo was as frank and open with his mother as when he had been a child; she had shared all his hopes and fears during his long time of probation, and now she shared his joy, and was soon coaxed back to cheerfulness, as he told her more of what had passed at the Casa Bella. She was quite herself again as she went in to dinner upon his arm, her grief was forgotten, she laughed merrily at his account of Enrico's philosophical counsels, and felt a glow of pride and happiness as she looked across the table at the son who had been all in all to her for so many years. Carlo was too happy to be hungry, but he pledged his mother over a bottle of Orvieto, and they drank Francesca's health, and clinked glasses, and made merry.

The *tête-à-tête* dinner at the Casa Bella was quieter, but happy, too, in its way. The old Captain beamed silently from behind the sirloin. Francesca looked radiant. They talked fitfully of the weather, of the orange-crop, of the silkworms, of the last letter from England—of everything, in fact, except the one subject that was nearest their hearts; but, then, old Dino was waiting, and it behoved them to keep up appearances. Their tongues were unloosed by the appearance of Sibyl and the dessert, and the disappearance of the servant.

'Sibyl,' said the Captain, taking the little

girl on his knee, 'what would you think if we were to have a wedding here?'

'A wedding, father?' Sibyl clapped her hands with delight. 'Oh, may I be the bride, father? May I be the bride?'

'No,' said the father, laughing, 'that character is bespoken. You will have to be my little housekeeper. Francesca is to be bride. There, you must drink her health: Long life and happiness to the future Signora Donati.'

Sibyl obediently repeated the words, but made a wry face over the claret.

'What horrid stuff, Daddy; do give me a bit of your orange, quick.' Then, with her mouth very full, 'But Fran can't be Signora Donati.'

'Oh, yes, she can when she marries Carlo,' said the Captain.

'Marries Carlo?' echoed Sibyl, in astonishment. 'Dear me, will Carlo be married? What a bother! I suppose he'll never play games and be jolly any more?'

'Why not?' said Francesca, laughing.

'Oh, he won't,' said Sibyl, looking wise and

elderly, 'I know he won't; I asked nurse the other day what it meant to be married, and she said it was when people grew steady and settled down.'

The two elders laughed heartily.

'But he will be your brother, you know, Sibyl, and brothers always play,' said Francesca.

'Carlo my brother?'

'Your brother-in-law.'

'Oh, yes, I know about that—that's what he had put on his cards,' said Sibyl, triumphantly; 'so he must have known he was going to be my brother before he came here; Dino said that long word was in-law.'

Then before Captain Britton had done laughing, Sibyl convulsed her companions by solemnly raising the glass to her lips again, and repeating in the gravest way imaginable,—

'Long life and many games to my future brother—in-law.'

Francesca was eager to go in quickly to see Signora Donati, but she had to wait till Sibyl was tucked up in bed and her father had finished his after-dinner nap. Then she threw a white, woolly shawl about her head and shoulders, slipped her arm into the Captain's, and crossed over to the Villa Bruno. The Signora was alone; she came forward to meet them with the prettiest little greeting imaginable. Francesca loved her dearly, and returned her embraces with all possible warmth; but above the soft and tender assurances of the Signora's delight in the news which Carlo had brought her, she was conscious of her lover's voice singing out in the garden. The joyous ring about the old Neapolitan song, the unmistakable rapture of the singer, filled her heart with happiness. The sweet, familiar air always brought back to her memory that first perfect evening at the Villa Bruno.

'He has done nothing but sing since he came back from you,' said the Signora, as the singer drew nearer, every word distinctly heard in that clear atmosphere:

> '*O dolce Napoli,*
> *O suol beato*
> *Dove sorridere*
> *Volle il creato,*
> *Tu sei l' impero*
> *Dell' armonia,*
> *Santa Lucia! Santa Lucia!*'

The last note still echoed in the air as Carlo stepped into the dimly-lighted room through the open window, bearing in his hand a bunch of red roses and myrtle-blossom. It was the picture he had so often imagined which met his gaze, for Francesca stood beside his mother, the lamplight shedding a soft glow over her sweet, fair face. She was dressed in some kind of soft white dress which made him think of a baby's robe, her wavy brown hair was a little ruffled by the white shawl which she had thrown aside, in her sweet, pure happiness she was exquisite.

'I did not know you had come,' he exclaimed, hastening towards her; 'how was it I never heard you?'

'We came without ceremony, there was no ringing of bells,' said Francesca.

'And Carlo was singing at the top of his voice,' said the mother, laughing. 'I foresee, Francesca, that he will now be like my canary, who is so happy that he sings all day long, and I have sometimes to extinguish him.'

'We have been wondering what Signor Piale

will say,' replied Francesca, smiling; 'you know he looks upon love as the supreme obstacle in the way of art.'

'Then he should not compose music to such words as these,' said Carlo, taking up a song from the open piano.

'Is that his last? I have not heard it,' said Francesca. 'Ah, he has dedicated it to me as he promised.'

'Go and sing it, Carlo; it suits you well,' said his mother.

'I am not well acquainted with your Tennyson,' she continued, turning to Captain Britton, 'but it seems to me that these words are melodious and well adapted for music.'

The Captain was not poetical, but he at once launched into an account of how he had once met the Laureate at Lord Blamton's, while Carlo and Francesca wandered off to the piano, Francesca glancing through the accompaniment to see if she could manage it.

Even in that land of beautiful voices Carlo Donati's voice was most remarkable. But Piale was the only person who quite knew what it was worth, and he had issued strict orders that his pupil was to sing nowhere save at home and at his lessons. He knew well enough that if Carlo once sang at a Neapolitan party he would be allowed no peace, but would become the spoilt and overworked amateur, and fail altogether to do justice to the severe but excellent training which he had now almost completed. The voice was a baritone of unusual power and sweetness; Piale's music suited the pathetic words admirably:

> 'Love is come with a song and a smile,
> Welcome love with a smile and a song;
> Love can stay but a little while.
> Why cannot he stay? They call him away;
> Ye do him wrong, ye do him wrong;
> Love will stay for a whole life long.'

The song ended, Francesca sat dreamily playing over the refrain which her lover had declaimed so passionately; he stood close to her, deftly arranging the flowers he had brought from the garden in her hair and dress. Then, after the thanks and praises of the listeners had been spoken, Captain Britton once more enlarged upon his meeting with the Laureate, and Carlo, foreseeing that the topic would last some time, looked longingly out into the dusky garden, then down at Francesca.

'The paths are quite dry, it is starlight,' he said: 'will you not come out?'

She smiled and nodded, let him wrap the white shawl about her, and crossed the room to the window. Carlo lingered a moment to slip a cluster of red roses into his mother's hand.

'We go into the garden for a few minutes, *madre mia*,' he explained.

She smiled approvingly, perceiving that he meant to claim all the liberty which an English betrothal permits, and then turned again to the Captain with a question, in her pretty broken English, which she was well aware would keep him happy for some time to come.

'And this Lord Blamton, at whose house it occurred, is he your friend?'

The lovers, supremely indifferent to both Lords and Laureates, strolled out into the starlit garden. All was still and peaceful; through the olives they could catch glimpses of the yellow lights in Pozzuoli, and every now and then a lurid crimson flame and a column of vapour lit up by the fierce glare, revealed in the distance the conical form of Vesuvius and its peaceful neighbour, Somma. There was a delicious fragrance in the air; thyme, and myrtle, and mignonette, filled the dewy garden with their sweetness; everywhere the peace of a great content seemed to brood. A stranger might have fancied something disturbing and incongruous in the burning mountain; but to Carlo Vesuvius was an old friend, not a terror. In his childhood he had fancied it a sort of symbol of the Deity, vaguely connecting it with that other pillar of cloud by day and pillar of fire by night of which old Father Cristoforo had told him. Not a care, not the least shadow of anxiety, broke the bliss—the unclouded happiness of that evening.

Remembering Enrico's advice to keep his happiness to himself, Carlo took a holiday, and stayed at home till the end of the week, when, partly prompted by a conscientious wish to break the news to Piale, and to keep his usual appointment with the old Maestro on Saturday morning, partly because he wished to search for a betrothal ring to his mind, he ordered his horse and rode in to Naples.

Pialo lived over a shop in the Strada Mont' Oliveto. His apartments were furnished in a Spartan manner without the least attempt at comfort or picturesqueness. A marble floor, unrelieved by carpet or mat, walls painted in pale green, but bare of a single picture, a grand piano in the middle of the room, a table strewn with music-paper, books, and pens, and a few straight-backed chairs stiffly set round it, completed the furniture of this musical anchorite. When Carlo entered the room that morning he found the old man poring over the score of some opera, his shaggy grey hair tossed back from his broad forehead, and the shabbiness of his many-coloured dressing-gown fully revealed by the sunshine which streamed in through the half-open *jalousies*. He looked up as Carlo entered, giving him a sharp, searching glance, as though to discover how the world went with him that morning. Convinced by the radiant happiness of his pupil's face that at present the sky was cloudless, he grunted out a rather surly 'Buon giorno,' and closed his book with an air of reluctance.

'I want your congratulations, Maestro,' said Carlo, coming quickly forward. 'Nothing but the most filial obedience and respect to yourself brought me away from my paradise this morning. You must mingle with praise your good wishes for our health and happiness.'

'Hein!' exclaimed the old man, pretending not to catch his meaning. 'You are an *avvocato*, I understand; young Ritter told me as much as that. *Corpo di Bacco!* don't come to me for congratulations. You've mistaken your profession. You are wasting—yes, wasting, the noblest gift of God.'

'But, Maestro, reflect; how is it possible for me to use my voice as you would have me? Would you wish me to leave my mother? And then, moreover, there are other considerations— I am about to be married.'

'Married!' The Maestro turned away with a groan. 'Ah, then I wash my hands of you! You are lost to art—lost to the noblest of the professions! Farewell to my hopes! All my efforts with you are thrown away! You might have been the pride of my old age and the delight of Europe. Instead you choose the career of a lawyer and the caresses of a woman.'

'You speak scornfully, Maestro,' replied the culprit, laughing. 'I shall add two adjectives to your bald remark—"the useful career," and "a perfect woman." Why, signor, you who know Miss Britton should be ready to make excuse for me. What else could you expect? Is the Muse of Harmony to take precedence of such an one?'

'Hear him!' cried Piale, in despair, 'great Heaven! and it is this ungrateful one that thou hast endowed with the voice of a seraph and the dramatic power of a Salvini!'

'My apologies to Salvini,' said Carlo, laughing merrily, 'but that, beloved Maestro, is bathos —a fine example.'

His laughter was so infectious that Piale was obliged to join in it, then, with a shrug of the shoulders, he shuffled across to the piano.

'You are incorrigible! I wash my hands

of you! But since you are in so jocular a mood at the prospect of settling down to so monotonous a life——'

'Maestro!' broke in Carlo, with indignation.

'Do I speak unadvisedly?' said Piale, with sarcasm; 'not at all. Oh, I know well enough what it will be. You will sit under your vine and under your fig-tree, and you will count the olive-branches round your table——'

'Signor Piale!'

'And you will say as you look, "I must work hard," and you will become the speaking-machine of the Neapolitan criminals, and you will use that divine gift for the proclamation of lies, and you will debase your fine dramatic genius and make it the tool of the worthless and the guilty. Since all this makes you in so gay a humour, come sing me your song from *Il Barbiere*.'

Pursing up his lips the old professor began to play the accompaniment of *Largo al Factotum*; and Carlo, entering into the spirit of the thing, and with his sense of humour touched by the analogy between the barber's glorification of his profession and the words that had just passed, sang magnificently.

At the end there was unbroken silence. The old professor sat lost in thought, Carlo watched him with a smile on his lips. Then, sauntering across the room, sang, *sotto voce*, the recitative which followed, throwing malicious meaning into the

'*Ah! Che bella vita! Oh! Che mestiere!*'

'It could not have been better sung!' cried Piale, with a gesture of despair. 'Carlo, perhaps I have dealt unfairly by you. I have never praised you, never told you what I thought of your powers; I feared to ruin that modesty which has endeared you to me. But now it is time that you seriously consider the matter. There, there, don't interrupt me! Marry if you will, and let your wife tend the Signora Donati in your absence. But do not allow so glorious a gift to rust unused.'

'But, dear Maestro,' said Carlo, gravely, 'you do not realise that others do not think of the profession as you do. Captain Britton regards the theatre as the school for hell, the stage is an abomination to him. He fancies that all actors are like that villain Merlino. And, indeed, it is wonderful that he made no objection to having as son-in-law one who is so deeply compromised as I am. I suppose he hardly realised the fact, he has almost forgotten poor Nita's existence.'

At the recollection of that sorrowful past he sighed. Piale was quick to note how the remembrance interfered with his present happiness.

'Well, only a brute would dream of holding you responsible for the sins of others,' he said, warmly.

'Tell me,' said Carlo, 'have you seen any mention of my sister lately in any of the musical papers?'

'I heard that Merlino's company had been in America for the last two years, and that Madame Merlino had made a good impression there. . . . Well, I suppose I must say no more, lad, but it is hard on a master to have his best pupil lost to the world.'

He changed the subject rather hastily. He

could not bear to bring back that cloud to Carlo's brow by telling him the last news of his sister.

His lesson over, Carlo began to ransack the jewellers' shops, and having at last found a broad gold gipsy ring with a single diamond which satisfied him he bent his steps towards his uncle's house, conscious that Guido Donati—a rather autocratic man—would require early notice of his nephew's engagement.

The interview passed off well. Uncle Guido thoroughly approved of the marriage, and treated his nephew in the most generous and paternal way, and Carlo came forth in excellent spirits. All seemed to promise well for his future life. Happy in his love, with the prospect of a fair inheritance, a hope which practically amounted to certainty of success in his profession, and with the best of mothers and the truest of friends, it seemed as if life could offer him nothing more. His face was radiant as he greeted Enrico Ritter.

'Well met!' he exclaimed, waylaying Enrico, who, in a fit of abstraction, would have passed him by.

'Oh, it is you!' exclaimed Enrico, looking him critically in the face. 'Well, what news?'

'You will be requested to dance at my wedding before long,' said Carlo, gaily.

'So!' Enrico whistled.

'I took your advice, you see, *amico mio*, and stayed at home, that you might not be afflicted with the trouble of congratulating me.'

'Yes, yes,' said Enrico, with a sarcastic smile. 'That is your kind way of putting it—egoist that you are! You stayed to enjoy yourself, and now you want to make me believe that you were considering my comfort and not your own. An egoist! A double-dyed egoist!'

But his laughter was suddenly checked. They were passing a hoarding in the Strada S. Trinità, Carlo had glanced at one of the placards, and now he clutched his friend's arm.

'Enrico!' he gasped; 'my sister's name—I thought I saw it. Look for me; I can't.'

Huge black letters on a pink ground danced in wild confusion before his eyes; but surely it was that hateful name of Merlino which had suddenly darkened his sky, which had struck a blow at his heart and left him stunned and bewildered!

'Dear old fellow, you must come on,' said Enrico. 'I didn't know those cursed placards would be out yet; but it is true, alas! only too true.'

Carlo walked on mechanically, feeling as though he were in a nightmare. His thoughts flew wildly from Francesca to Anita, from his mother to Captain Britton, from his uncle to Merlino. He had no definite ideas, only a giddy consciousness that the world, so bright but a minute before, was now overshadowed, and that a nameless fear filled his heart.

'Where?' he faltered, after a brief silence.

'The Mercadante,' said Enrico, following his train of thought and understanding the laconic question as a friend should.

'Let us come there,' said Carlo.

Enrico silently complied. After a time his friend looked up with another question,—

'You knew of this before, then?'

Enrico signed an assent.

'The day I last saw you?' he added, after a pause.

'What? That thing you tore out of the *Piccolo*? Why did you try to keep it from me?'

'I wanted you to have a cloudless betrothal,' said Enrico, rather reluctantly.

'Ah, *amico mio!*' exclaimed the other, gratefully. 'You shield me thus, and then call yourself egoist!'

'Of course,' said Enrico, who hated to be caught in a kindly action. 'It was pure egoism. Naturally, I wish you to be happy, for it disturbs me and makes me uncomfortable to see you as you are now. Purely for my own sake I deferred the evil day.'

Carlo could not help smiling, even then, at the energy with which his friend tried to establish his own selfishness for the sake of triumphing in his pet theory.

'I must find out whether they are yet in Naples,' he said, growing grave once more, and trying hard to collect his thoughts. 'Oh, Enrico, how shall I break the news to my mother? She is unfit to bear the least shock.'

'I would keep it from her, then—at any rate, till you know what line your sister intends to take,' said Enrico. 'But, see, we are close to the Mercadante. Shall I make inquiries for you?'

'I wish you would,' said Carlo, with a look of relief. 'Ask when the Company arrives in Naples, and where they are to be found.'

Enrico walked forward, Carlo following more slowly; on past two open-air *caffès*, with groups of idlers beneath a shady trellis-work of vine and euonymus; on past a stall gaily wreathed with lemons and greenery, where thirsty Neapolitans were drinking mineral water; on till the arsenal was in sight, and the red tower of the lighthouse, while in the foreground was the Teatro Mercadante. Little had he thought that the sight of its pink walls with their white facings would ever have caused him such strange emotion. Huge placards were posted here in all directions. He read them over and over in a sort of dream, taking in little but that one name in larger type, 'MME. MERLINO.' At length, Enrico came forth, having made his inquiries.

'They do not seem to know the exact date of

their arrival,' he said, in answer to Carlo's mute question. 'The man was just going off to his *siesta*, and was not best pleased at being hindered. However, he wrote down the address for me. You will find them there, whenever they do arrive. It may be to-morrow or any day next week. They are coming from America, but by what route the fellow didn't know. However, you see by the placards there are no performances for another ten days.'

Carlo took the paper, and read the address.

'I shall be here again to-morrow,' he said. 'I will call and see if they have arrived, and till then I shall say nothing to my mother.'

'That would be wise,' said Enrico. 'Then she will be spared the worry and uncertainty. You look tired, *amico mio*. Come home with me, and have your *siesta* in peace.'

'No,' said Carlo; 'I want to go home. I want to tell Francesca.'

'You can't ride back in this heat; you'll get a sunstroke.'

But he only shook his head, and, with an unmistakable air of wishing to be alone, said good-bye to his friend, and went to order his horse.

Enrico turned to look after him. Profound dejection was expressed in his walk. The serpent had all too soon invaded his paradise.

CHAPTER V.

A THREATENING SKY.

'Come, all ye faithful, come, and dare to prove
The bitter sweet, the pain and bliss of love.'
TRENCH.

FRANCESCA came down one of the shady garden paths to meet her lover; she held in her hand a forked branch, on which, nestled among the pale green leaves, grew four fresh-looking lemons. For a moment Carlo forgot everything in the bliss of seeing her again. It seemed to him that they had been ages apart; that he had been toiling across a barren desert to reach this cool, green retreat, in which his betrothed reigned supreme. How beautiful she looked in that familiar, soft, white dress, and with her white forehead and delicate colouring shaded by a large hat! The hat was one of those shallow white ones which can sometimes be bought for two or three *soldi;* it was not calculated, however, to sustain the embraces of a lover, and it speedily fell back, leaving Francesca with her wavy brown hair uncovered. For a minute, Carlo held her from him, that he might the better see her, with a datura-tree for background, and the soft, creamy flowers drooping over her head. Francesca, having known him and loved him for years, saw in one glance that he was in trouble.

'You are tired, my own,' she said. 'It was too hot for you to ride back so early; you should have taken your *siesta* at Naples.'

'I couldn't rest,' he said, with a sigh. 'I wanted to get back to you.'

'Something has grieved you. Does Uncle Guido disapprove of our betrothal?'

'No, oh no. How could he do that? He treated me as though I had been his son.'

'Yet something or someone has been troubling you. But we will not talk of it now; you shall rest first. Come into the Rose-room; it will be cool there, and the sun is not off the summer-house yet.'

They went together towards the house. The Rose-room was Francesca's own little sitting-room.

It had a ceiling painted after the Italian fashion with wreaths of pink roses; it had cool grey walls crowded with a most miscellaneous collection of photographs and water-colour sketches; it had rose-coloured curtains in figured muslin; and, after the manner of rooms, it betrayed its owner's chief failing—it was in wild disorder. Francesca was by no means immaculate; like other girls, she had her faults, and untidiness was one of them.

'Try my rocking-chair,' she said, removing a guitar which reposed upon the cushions, and trying to find a home for it upon the crowded table. 'I will be back directly.'

Carlo, rescuing the guitar, which was in imminent danger of falling, lay back in the easy chair, and waited, letting his hands wander idly about among the strings. It was sweet to feel already so entirely at home at Casa Bella—its very confusion was dear to him. Presently Francesca returned, bearing a big tumbler of St. Galmier, which she set down upon Dante's *Paradiso*, while she selected the finest of the lemons from her branch.

'Lend me your knife, Carlino,' she said; 'I've lost mine, as usual. There!' as she cut open the cool, ripe fruit; 'isn't that a beauty? How much, I wonder, for this glassful? I should think half. Ah, how like me! I've forgotten the sugar.' Then, running to the door, 'Sibyl! Sibyl!'

The little sister came flying down the passage.

'Run and fetch me some sugar, will you, Sibyl dear? Oh, bother! Now, what have I done with the store-room key? Look, darling, I think it must be on my dressing-table, or, perhaps, in the pocket of my blue gown; or, if not, in my work-basket.'

Sibyl ran away to hunt for the missing key, and Francesca searched among the contents of the table to see if by chance it had been left there.

'Ah, Carlo *mio!*' she said, with a pretty penitence, 'I fear I am not, as the ladies say who advertise in the newspapers, "thoroughly domesticated." I shall have to mend my evil ways now.'

Carlo pretended not to understand what

'domesticated' meant, and they had much merriment over a dictionary, which declared that it was to be 'tame' and 'not foreign.'

Sibyl at last returned with the sugar-basin, claiming one lump as wages and accepting another to run away. Then Francesca began to stir the contents of the tumbler with an ivory paper-knife since spoons were not handy; and in much laughter and lover-like teasing Carlo forgot all about the cloud-shadow which had arisen.

The ring fitted to perfection, and Francesca's delight was pretty to see; she was not above a womanly weakness for jewellery, and frankly owned that she always had longed for just one diamond.

'And what about the old Maestro?' she exclaimed at last. 'You never told me how he bore the news.'

'Well, dear old Piale was, or pretended to be, a good deal depressed. It seems that he really had set his heart on my going on the stage, and had not at all realised how impossible that would be.'

'Yet you do not feel as my father does about theatre-going?' said Francesca. 'And Clare! Don't you remember what arguments we used to have with dear Clare about it?'

'Yes, she was dead against it; but then she was brought up in a Puritan family, and the old prejudices lingered with her. For me, I have no feeling whatever of that sort, but nevertheless the life of an operatic singer is quite the last I should willingly choose. Piale talks scoffingly of the humdrum life of an advocate; but for my part I shall be very well content to stay at home, with the hope of some day following in my father's steps and doing a little for the country. Think of the wretchedness of a wandering life! It's all very well to talk about delighting Europe —practically one would be little better than an exile—and into the bargain Piale owns that art requires the sacrifice of domestic life.'

'I knew he would not approve of me,' said Francesca, laughing. 'We must have him to our wedding, Carlo, and he shall make a speech. What fun he will be!'

Just for a minute, as they talked of theatrical

life, Carlo's thoughts had reverted to Nita, but Francesca's reference to the wedding soon dispersed the cloud. He had most markedly the Italian faculty of living wholly in the present, and enjoying it much as a child enjoys life. They lingered long in the Rose-room. Later on, when the heat of the afternoon was past, they walked through the garden and down the vine-clad slopes to the beach, where old Florestano sat smoking his pipe with his back against a boat. He sprang up, on seeing them, as quickly as his rheumatism would permit.

'Going for a row, signor?' he said, when he had finished his lengthy congratulations, and had made Francesca blush deliciously.

'Yes,' said Carlo, flinging his coat into the stern; 'but we shan't want you, Florestano; we shall never want you any more,' and, with a laugh, he shoved the boat down to the water's edge.

'Ah, signorina,' said the old fisherman, chuckling, 'he is one to be proud of, that he is. Why, I do declare he might be a fisherman. Look at him now.'

And with delighted pride the old man watched

the skill with which the strong, active figure in straw hat and shirt-sleeves set to work. Carlo looked round with a bright, glowing face. 'Come, Francesca, let us be off. Good-bye, Florestano. Ah, wait a minute, though! Have a cigar?'

He handed his case to the old fisherman, who helped himself with a smiling face, then he shoved the boat into the water, sprang in, and, taking the oars, rowed off towards Ischia.

The fisherman stood on the quiet and lonely beach watching them, and meditatively stroking one of his huge, projecting ears.

'Well, well,' he remarked, shrugging his shoulders, 'some of us be born to happiness and some to sorrow, there's no helping that. But all of us ought to be born to a fair chance of living somehow. So says the young signor, but I doubt me if, for all his hot words and his seeming near as much of a Socialist as any of us, he'd care to act it out in his life. Eh, eh! we be all of us ready enough to talk about others, but to live for them that's another matter.'

And, with a grim chuckle, Florestano pulled

out a number of *La Campana* from his pocket, and, stretching himself on the pebbles, began to spell out more lessons in Socialism.

The sun was low in the heavens when the lovers returned from their row. Carlo had to hasten home to his mother, but later in the evening he once more appeared at Casa Bella. Apart from Francesca all his restless apprehension had returned.

Captain Britton was asleep in the dining-room. Francesca was in the dusky drawing-room seated at the piano, where two candles under rose-coloured shades made a little oasis of light. She was trying over her favourite of all Carlo's songs, '*Dio Possente*,' but broke off with a little cry of surprise and delight as he came towards her.

'I shall think that my ring is a fairy ring,' she cried, 'and brings me all I wish for. I was just longing to hear you sing this.'

Carlo had not felt in a singing humour, but her words drove everything else from his mind, and he sang perhaps all the better for the real care and anxiety which were oppressing him, certainly he sang as she had never before heard him sing.

'Piale is right,' she said at the close, brushing away the tears from her eyes; 'nature meant you for a singer; you were Valentino then, and no one else.'

Carlo did not speak; she looked up at him quickly, and again saw that look of care which he had borne back with him from Naples.

'My darling,' she said, making room for him on the ottoman beside her, 'you are keeping something from me; you are unhappy, Carlo *mio*, and yet you will not let me know.'

'Yes,' he said sadly, 'I must let you know; that is what I came back for. You remember Nita?'

'Your sister? Yes,—oh, yes. What of her? Has she written?'

'No, but to-day in Naples, as I walked down the Strada S. Trinità, I saw that she was to sing the week after next at the Mercadante.'

Francesca looked startled. All in a minute it flashed upon her that the perfect peace of their betrothal was disturbed, and that it could never return.

She knew enough of Nita's story to be aware how painful it would be for both Signora Donati and Carlo to have her as the prima donna of a Neapolitan theatre; but she tried hard to see gleams of possible good in the news.

'She may be sorry, and come to see you,' she suggested. 'Oh, surely she would come back to Villa Bruno when she is so near to it as Naples?'

But Carlo was not hopeful. She listened to all his doubts and fears with tender, womanly sympathy. She was no spoilt child caring only for the pleasure of her betrothal; perhaps, indeed, notwithstanding the ruffled peace, she had never been so happy as she was that evening when Carlo told her his troubles, and then, with his arm round her, whispered sweet words about the comfort of telling her.

Francesca quite agreed with Enrico that it would be better to say nothing as yet to the Signora Donati; and even in her anxiety there was keen pleasure in feeling that she had a right to share her lover's cares.

The next day was Sunday, and Carlo, as usual,

drove in to the English church with the Brittons. But after the service he left them, pleading an engagement, and went off to see if Merlino's Company had arrived.

The Palazzo Forti was in a gloomy side street, he entered the courtyard, and found his way up a very dirty staircase to the third floor, where he rang and inquired whether Madame Merlino had arrived. An answer in the affirmative from a bright-eyed little servant made his heart leap into his throat. He had not expected it. He had walked to the old Palazzo in the firm conviction that his sister would not yet have reached Naples, and to be told that she was actually close to him almost took away his breath. He hesitated a moment.

'Is she within? can I see her?' he inquired.

The servant seemed a little doubtful, but said she would ask, and, taking Carlo's card, she disappeared, leaving him in the doorway. In all his life he had never felt so uncomfortable. He had never known Anita well; her convent education had made her practically a stranger to him, and now years had passed since their last meeting, and between them was the shadow of her wrong-doing. Then, too, he was not even sure whether he should see her alone, her husband might be there; and Carlo, being Italian and hot-tempered, was not quite sure how the sight of Merlino might affect him. He breathed quickly as the servant returned.

'Would the Signor step this way for a minute?'

Setting his teeth, he followed the maid down a passage, and was ushered into a good-sized but comfortless-looking room. He was surprised and relieved to find within it neither his sister nor Merlino, but a young Englishman of about eight-and-twenty with fair hair and moustache, arched eyebrows, and keen light blue eyes, in which there was no mistaking the sparkle of genuine wit; but the face was a restless one, and the expression of careless good-humour was sometimes slightly tinged with bitterness. He bowed, then glanced again at the visitor with undisguised curiosity.

'You are Madame Merlino's brother, I think?'

Carlo assented.

'I should have known you anywhere, the likeness is so strong.'

'I speak English, if you prefer it, sir,' said Carlo, noticing that the stranger's Italian was far from fluent.

'Do you? that will be a great relief, then. The patience of you foreigners amazes me. How you can learn our barbarous tongue I can't conceive. For me, I only learnt enough of yours to satisfy my singing-master.'

'May I ask whom I am speaking to?' said Carlo.

'I am Sardoni—that, at least, is my professional name—*primo tenore* of "the happy band of pilgrims" who patrol this wicked world under Merlino's care. When they brought me your card just now I thought I might ask to see you, although Madame Merlino is out, for, to tell the truth, signor, it is quite time that Madame Merlino's friends and relations did something to save her. You must pardon the liberty I am taking, but, indeed, it is little use mincing matters in an affair of this kind.'

Carlo took a long look at the speaker. He was evidently an English gentleman—a man doubtless with faults enough, but yet, he instinctively felt, a man to be trusted.

'My sister is out, you say,' he began, with a troubled look.

'She went out driving this morning,' said Sardoni, promptly, 'with her usual cavalier, Comerio, our first baritone. But I know Comerio well, and he will not long be content to be a mere hanger-on. Every day Madame Merlino gets more under that man's power. He and she——'

But here he hastily broke off, for Carlo sprang forward with a gesture so threatening that anyone but an Englishman would have recoiled a pace.

'Be silent!' he thundered; 'how dare you couple my sister's name with the name of that brute?'

His dark eyes were all ablaze with anger. Sardoni was silent, not because he doubted the truth of his own words, but because he was obliged to pause and admire.

'I see you are the brother whom Madame Merlino needs,' he said, quietly; 'and it is in order that those two names may not with just cause be coupled together all the world over that I speak to you plainly.'

The glow of colour had faded from Carlo's face, and had left him unusually pale. He turned away with a groan as Sardoni ended. Vaguely as he had dreaded his sister's arrival, he had never dreamed that it would be so bad as this.

'Her husband?' he said at length.

'Merlino is a brute, but many degrees better than Comerio. 'Tis a sort of lion and unicorn business, with your sister for crown. But you spoke as though you knew Comerio?'

'I only know what report has to say of him,' replied Carlo. 'He was singing here five years ago; his wife and children, I believe, still live here.'

'Report says nothing of him that is not strictly true.'

'But how is it, then, that Merlino is so blind to his own interests as to keep him in his troupe?'

'I can't say, unless it is that tyrants always believe in their own superiority. And then, too,

Comerio is such a wily devil, he always manages to keep in Merlino's good books. There has never been the least apparent reason for getting rid of him; and, besides, Merlino is not so overburdened with wealth that he can afford to cancel an engagement. Italian opera is not such a paying concern as people think.'

'I must try to see my sister,' said Carlo, with a sigh, 'or write to her.'

'Then if you see her allow me to suggest that you do not call on her here, where ten to one you will fall foul of her husband; and if you write, do so now and entrust the letter to me, for Merlino watches her correspondence with lynx eyes, and does not scruple to open every letter.'

Carlo uttered an impatient exclamation of disgust. Every sentence which the Englishman let fall seemed to reveal to him a fresh glimpse of the intolerable life which poor Nita was leading. He accepted the pen and ink which his companion offered him, however, and, drawing a chair to the table, began with deepening colour to write.

Sardoni glanced at him from time to time; he had taken up a newspaper, and made as though he were reading it, but in reality his mind was full of his Italian visitor. Carlo's face was almost as easy to read as a book, and Sardoni could not help feeling sorry for him. He had just witnessed one of the most painful sights imaginable, that of a perfectly unsullied nature being brought for the first time into near connection with a network of evil. There was something, too, in the implicit trust which Donati had reposed in him which appealed to him strongly. What a wretched position to be in! Powerless to help his own sister without trusting to the help and believing in the honesty of a stranger and a foreigner! Carlo in the meantime had finished his letter, and, folding it up, handed it unsealed to Sardoni.

The Englishman put it in his pocket-book, remarking, as he did so, 'For a perfect stranger you trust me with a good deal, Signor Donati.'

Carlo looked troubled as it flashed across him how unsuspiciously he had believed the stranger's words. It had never occurred to him that Sardoni could possibly have any reason for misleading him. He looked at him searchingly.

'But then, you are an Englishman,' he said, in a tone of relief.

Sardoni laughed. 'That is a compliment to my nation which I shall not readily forget. But look here,' an expression of great bitterness stole over his face, 'there are many of my own countrymen who would snap their fingers at my word of honour.'

Carlo again looked him through and through, and, as he looked, the blue eyes seemed to grow less hard, to appeal against that harsh opinion which had just been mentioned.

'Oh, as for that,' said Carlo, with the expressive gestures of a Neapolitan, 'that is just nothing at all to me. I trust you, signor.'

Sardoni smiled and grasped his hand.

'I'll not betray your confidence,' he said.

And with that the two men parted.

Carlo went down the dirty stone stairs, looking pale and harassed. Sardoni with a flushed face returned to his newspaper, but still did not take in one word.

'He trusted me,' he thought to himself—'he really did trust me. Oh, God! if I could only change natures with a fellow like that!' Then, as some painful recollection brought hot tears to his eyes, he sprang up, and flinging aside his newspaper strode across to the piano and began to play a waltz. 'You are a fool, Jack! a fool! a fool! Why should that Italian make you think of it? A mere countrified innocent!'

And with that he played on recklessly, doing his best to forget Donati's eyes.

CHAPTER VI.

THE STORM BREAKS.

'God be praised, that to believing souls
Gives light in darkness, comfort in despair.'
King Henry VI., Part II.

How to break the news to his mother? this was Carlo's sole thought as he walked home on that Sunday afternoon. For an Italian he was an unusually good walker, having fallen a good deal into English habits through his close friendship with the Brittons; and perhaps it was to the free country life which he had always lived, and to his daily rides to and from Naples, that he owed his brilliant colouring and his healthy mind and body.

It tortured him to think that the story which had been a shock to him would be tenfold worse to his mother. It had been, as Sardoni observed, his first near connection with evil, but to his mother it would be the first introduction to evil at all. He had not lived the life of a Neapolitan student without coming across many Comerios; but his mother, in her peaceful country life, her tranquil invalid existence, knew nothing of wickedness. His mind was so taken up with the difficulty of telling her that he had no leisure to think of the yet greater difficulty, how to help Anita.

He could not bear to be the one to bring her these bad tidings; he half thought of asking Father Cristoforo to go to her; then, ashamed of shrinking from a painful task, he forced himself to pass the old man's house and climbed the hill, turning over in his mind a dozen different ways of approaching the subject, and feeling satisfied with none of them.

There was something very beautiful in the devotion of this mother and son; perhaps only Francesca and Clare knew how entirely Carlo had given his life to the work his father had left him, or how wonderfully it had helped to mould his character. To a woman it is second nature to devote herself to an invalid, nor does it involve any very serious break in her life; but to a man, obliged to go on with his daily work at the same time, the strain of attendance in a sick-room is infinitely greater. If he can live this life for years, it gives him an established habit of always ruling his life by the needs of another, and not by his own desires.

There were two gates to the grounds of Villa Bruno. The one nearest to Naples was that which led into the stable-yard, and Carlo, from force of custom, went in this way, although he was on foot. He was surprised to see a hired carriage in the yard; he wondered if possibly Frau Ritter had driven out to call on his mother, and paused on his way to the house to ask a servant who was the visitor.

'Oh, signor,' said the girl, flushing up, 'they say it is Madame Merlino!'

With an exclamation, which was almost a cry, he rushed on towards the house. His mother had had no preparation whatever—the shock might be fatal to her. And yet, surely it looked well that Nita should at once hurry home in this way? Surely that in itself gave the lie to Sardoni's assertion? And then it flashed across him that

Nita would regard him in the light of the elder brother in the story of the prodigal son, and he prayed that he might be his direct opposite.

Flinging open the front door he hurried on, pausing for an instant outside the *salotto*. There was a sound of voices; he hastily entered, glanced quickly towards his mother's couch, then towards his sister, who had risen at sight of him with a look so frightened and timid that he longed to reassure her, as one longs to still the fears of a terrified child.

'Why, Nita!' he exclaimed, kissing her repeatedly, 'I have been trying to find you in Naples, but you were before me after all.'

Something in the tone of his '*Ben venuto*,' and in the many untranslateable Italian phrases with which he greeted her, brought the tears to Anita's eyes.

She watched intently while Carlo bent down to kiss his mother.

'You are cold, *madre mia!*' he exclaimed. 'You are faint and over-tired.'

'Ah, it is my fault!' cried Nita, vehemently. 'It is I who have tired her and broken her heart!'

He saw that there would be no quieting her just then, and took the law into his own hands.

'You must rest a little,' he said; 'you too are tired; and then, after dinner, mother will be fit to talk again. See, I will show you a room—the place is a little altered.'

With some difficulty he enticed her away, but no sooner were they alone than her tears again broke forth.

'Oh, Carlo! I am afraid I have been too much for her,' she exclaimed, 'and yet—and yet—I wanted so to come.'

'Yes, yes, I am so glad you came; only we must be careful!' said poor Carlo, distracted at the thought that she was keeping him from his mother, and much alarmed as he recollected how white and weary the invalid had looked. 'There, you will lie down and rest till dinner-time, will you not?'

'But I ought to go back,' sobbed Nita.

'Not yet,' he said; 'you must dine first; and now promise me to rest. There, I will not stay longer; I am a little anxious—she is not strong, you know.'

He tore himself away, and returned as fast as possible to the *salotto*. His mother's face was hidden; he could hear her low, gasping sobs.

'*Madre mia!*' he cried, and there was anguish in his voice. 'Oh, do not give way! She has come back to us, *carina*—all will be well, if only you will take care of yourself.'

'I must tell you ——' she sobbed.

'Not now,' he said, 'not now, mother. Indeed you must be quiet or ——'

'I must speak,' she said, 'it is killing me! I must speak now, that you may promise me to save her.'

'From her husband?' he asked, anxious to find how much she knew.

'No, no—from one she loves. Don't look like that, Carlo—her husband was so stern and cruel, and she was afraid of him, and—and this man was kind.'

'Kind!' ejaculated Carlo, with scorn indescribable.

'He always tried to shield her from her husband, and then, when they were leaving

America, she was in debt and he lent her money, and ——'

'Enough, darling; enough,' he said with tenderness which contrasted strangely with his last ejaculation. 'She came and told you all, and now we can help her. If you love me, try to rest.'

But it was too late. The shock and the agitation had brought on one of the Signora's worst attacks. Carlo hastily summoned a servant, and the whole household came rushing together in a miserable confusion of helplessness. But the maids only glanced at their mistress's face and went away; they would have left their own relations rather than have stayed in a room where the Death Angel already hovered.

It was then, in his terrible, lonely watch, that Carlo thanked Heaven that Francesca was English. The doctor had already been sent for, but he left his mother for a moment and hurried towards the group of weeping women gathered round Anita.

'We have sent for Father Cristoforo, signor,' said one, hoping for a word of commendation for her forethought.

But Carlo took no notice, nor did his stern face soften.

'One of you go instantly,' he said, 'and fetch Miss Britton.'

Francesca knew little of sickness, nor had she ever seen death, but she had none of the Italian shrinking from a dying bed, in fact, every thought of herself was swallowed up in the one longing to be able to help Carlo. Cutting short the servant's tearful description of the Signora's state, she rushed out, not even pausing for a hat, and never stopped running till she reached the Villa Bruno. Then she pushed past the little group who would have detained her, knocked at the door of the *salotto*, and softly entered the room where, only a day or two before, they had spent such a happy evening.

For a moment she stood amazed, able to think of nothing but the havoc wrought in so short a time. Her lover knelt beside the couch, he looked ten years older than when they had parted that morning. The Signora, whose head rested on his arm, was haggard, ghastly, utterly changed, while the indescribable look of approaching death upon her face seemed reflected in the young face which bent over her.

'Darling, is there anything I can do?' said Francesca, when she had wiped the damp brow and reverently kissed the dying woman.

'Nothing,' he replied, 'except to stay here. You do not mind?' He looked up at her with questioning eyes, which yet were sure of their answer.

'Oh, no!' she said. 'I am so thankful you sent for me.'

A long sigh escaped him; he tried to stifle it, lest it should disturb his mother, who lay with closed eyes. And after that the room was perfectly quiet, so quiet that Francesca could hear the ticking of her watch; while the canary in the window, pecking the bars of his cage with his little pink beak, seemed to make a noise so loud that she wondered whether it would disturb the Signora.

At last there was a change in the wan face; the eyes opened, and the Signora looked up at Francesca with a smile.

Perhaps the beautiful face of the girl made

her think of her own daughter, for the smile changed to a look of anguish as she turned her eyes to her son.

'Don't forsake Nita—promise me—save her—try to save her.'

The words were gasped out with an agony of tone indescribable. But yet it was not till Carlo's answer was given that Francesca's eyes brimmed over with tears.

'I promise, *madre mia*—I promise.'

His face was like the face of a saviour, strong, pure, and sweet; his voice was firm and clear. No one could have helped trusting him.

A look of rest—even of hopefulness—stole over his mother's face. She lay still for a few minutes, then turned again to Francesca with a most beautiful smile.

'He has never given me one moment's sorrow all his life,' she said.

The words, which would be sweet to remember in after years, which might bring in time to the lips of the son a reflection of the mother's smile as she uttered them, were, just then, more than he could endure. His fortitude gave way; he had little to reproach himself with, yet it grieved him now to remember that at times it had been a hard struggle to leave Naples and return to the quiet of Villa Bruno, and that sometimes he had perhaps lingered a little longer than he should have done at Casa Bella. Now his days of service were over; she would no longer need his help.

With a cry, which tore Francesca's heart, he bent down, clasping the dying form yet closer as he sobbed out a passionate appeal,—

'Mother, mother, do not leave me!'

But the Signora was past hearing, past speaking—only she felt his close embrace, and, feebly raising her left hand, passed it behind his head with that gentle pressure—half caress, half support—which every woman knows how to bestow on a baby. And thus they stayed till the door opened, and the old priest and a little acolyte entered, barely in time to administer the last sacraments. Then Carlo regained his composure, stung into calmness by a sort of bitter resentment that an outsider must usurp those last sacred moments, and that he, heretic and alien, had no part or lot in the ceremony, and would be expected to leave the room. But Father Cristoforo, who was a son first and a Churchman afterwards, read his thoughts at once.

'Stay, my son,' he said, with so kind and fatherly a look, that Carlo's bitter thoughts were banished, and he knelt on, still supporting his mother.

Francesca knelt, too, on the other side of the couch, but she could neither pray nor feel; she watched the scene like one in a dream. The sunshine streamed in through the window, lighting up the white, unconscious face of the Signora and the grief-stricken face of her son, the rich vestments and tonsured head of the priest, the curious, roving eyes of the acolyte with his little silver-toned bell. But Francesca was still numb from the exceeding pain of watching her lover's agony. Now he was peaceful once more; his thoughts were raised above the pain of the parting, but her thoughts would not follow. The monotonous voice of Father Cristoforo, as he intoned the service, seemed only to increase her dull stupor. It was not till the canary in the window broke out into a sudden burst of song that her heart seemed to awake once more, and to join in the familiar words, '*Gloria in excelsis Deo. Et in terra pax hominibus.*' And then, as once more the service became unintelligible to her, she bent her head, and prayed on with fast-flowing tears, 'God! I thank Thee that she is spared the pain—that it is only left for us.'

When she looked up once more, all was over. Father Cristoforo, with a few kind words, went quietly away; from without there was a sound of bitter weeping; but Carlo knelt on with bowed head and peaceful heart, and the Signora's face was stamped with that calm majesty of death which Francesca had never before seen, and the canary in the window still sang his song of praise.

CHAPTER VII.

'NO ONE BUT YOU.'

'You like to behold and even to touch the Cross, but, alas! when the command comes to you to bear it!'—FÉNELON.

FRANCESCA had lived many years in Italy, and had more than once witnessed the passionate demonstrations of sorrow in a bereaved household; nevertheless, it was something of a shock to her to leave the quiet room of death and to go to Anita, whom she found surrounded by the weeping servants. They evidently took a melancholy pleasure in watching her violent paroxysms of grief.

To the English girl such a state of things seemed dreadful; she did as she would have been done by, and induced the noisy mourners to go away, thinking that poor Anita would find whatever comfort there was for her in silence and solitude. She could not understand that total absence of the consciousness of others, which to a northern nature is so utterly foreign, and she would have left Anita with a few tender words and a long, close embrace had not the poor girl clung to her like a child with such wild sobs and tears, such loud, unrestrained crying, that Francesca began to understand that she must be comforted much as Sibyl needed comforting after some dire disaster.

At length, words began to frame themselves amid the sobs, a constant repetition of the one bitter regret which overpowered everything else —'I have killed her! I have killed her! It is all my doing!'

'You could not tell—you could not know,' said Francesca, feeling it hard indeed to find words to meet so terrible a grief, and weeping, too, for sympathy. 'She has been so much weaker of late—unable to bear any shock—but how could you know? And, oh, Nita, she must have been so glad that you came!'

'No, no,' sobbed Nita. 'I might have stayed away, and then she would have forgotten.'

'Never, for she loved you,' said Francesca. 'Her last words almost were of you. Oh, if you could but have heard how she begged Carlo not to leave you!'

But at this Nita only wept the more.

'Carlo will hate me,' she cried. 'Oh, let me go! let me go! Tell them to put in the horses. I can't stay here any longer.'

'He does not hate you; he loves you,' said Francesca, warmly. 'He promised the Signora that he would always take care of you.'

Something in her tone quieted Nita. She lay musing over the words, wondering if, indeed, her brother knew all and would yet help her, trembling with fear at the thought of meeting him, and yet trembling still more when she thought of going back to Naples to face temptations too strong for her.

Francesca watched her tenderly, aware that some conflict was going on in her mind, though wholly ignorant of her story, and far too young and innocent to dream of the meaning which lay in the dying words of the Signora. Nita was in trouble, and in some sort of difficulty, and Carlo had promised to help her. Francesca did not curiously wonder what the difficulty might be, nor did she for one moment doubt Carlo's power of saving her. She accepted everything with the quiet confidence of a child who is vaguely conscious that there is trouble in the house, but is quite certain that its elders will soon make all right. Looking at Nita, she saw how strong a likeness existed between the brother and sister; and even if she had not felt drawn towards her before by her loneliness and her grief, this would have appealed to her. The fine profile and the warm, bright colouring, were exactly alike, but the mouth was disappointing, and had the same weakness which had slightly spoilt the expression of Signora Donati; while the eyes, though large and beautiful, were lacking in soul, and might almost have been the eyes of a doll, so little did they vary. But yet, as Nita lay there in her grief and self-reproach, trying to make up her mind between two evils, wondering which fear was the least intolerable, there was something about her which pleaded for pity. She was so young, so weak—a parasite by nature, she seemed ready to cling to anything, no matter what it was, so long as it had the strength which she lacked.

She was afraid of sleeping in the same house as her dead mother, but then she was yet more afraid of confessing to her husband where she had been. She dreaded meeting Carlo, but she still more dreaded meeting Comerio. All at once it occurred to her to wonder who her companion was.

'I have forgotten your name, signorina,' she said, looking into the sweet, pure face above her; 'but I think you must be Carlo's English playmate from Casa Bella?'

'Yes; I am Francesca Britton,' she replied, quietly, not liking just then to speak of her happy betrothal.

'Ah! how shocked I was in the old days at the games you and he played together!' said Nita, wistfully. 'And now—now it is I who have shocked you all. But you were quite right all the time. I have seen American life since then, and if we Italian girls had something of their liberty, there would not be so many broken hearts among us.'

The words reminded her of her grief, and she again burst into tears.

'Let me fetch Carlo,' said Francesca. 'He will comfort you as no one else can. Oh, you must not say you are afraid of him, that is only because you have forgotten. And I may tell him that you will stay, may I not?—you could not leave him all alone.'

Nita sobbed out something inarticulate, which Francesca took for a consent, and hurried away in search of her lover. She found him in the *salotto*, but the body of the Signora had been carried to her own room, and Carlo, looking broken-hearted, was trying to write a letter to his uncle to tell him the news. Softly passing her arm round his neck, and with her cool cheek leaning against his heated brow, she stood by him for some moments in silence.

'I must go home, my own,' she said, at length. 'Father will have come back, and will not know where I am. May I ask him to come in and see if he can help you in any way?'

Carlo thanked her. He felt dazed and bewildered; he thought it would be a comfort to have the help of the kind-hearted Englishman, who delighted in managing other people's affairs.

'And then there is Nita!' he exclaimed, with a look of perplexity. That promise which he had made returned to him. It lay like a heavy weight on his burdened mind; he had promised to save her, but how to perform that promise he had not an idea.

'It was about Nita I wanted to speak to you,' said Francesca. 'She said at first that she must go back to Naples at once, and seemed to dread meeting you. But I think—I really think she would stay if you went to her and let her see that you care for her still. She is in terrible distress, and no one but you can comfort her, Carlo mio.'

'No one but you!—No one but you!' The words haunted him as he turned to go to Nita. His mother had trusted all to him; Francesca, too, seemed to think that with him lay the sole chance of reaching his sister. Their very confidence seemed to crush him, he was utterly at a loss to know what he should do or say; he could not even feel acutely, sympathy seemed dead, his heart cold and numb with suffering, and yet, impelled by the truth of those words, 'No one but you!' he entered Nita's room. Her face was buried in the pillow, she was sobbing aloud, and took no notice of his presence. He sat down by the bed and mechanically took her hand in his; her sobs did not move him, and no words of comfort came to his lips.

But all at once, as he watched the little hand which lay in his, a keen pang of pain shot through his heart. The hand was like his mother's hand, so much like that he could hardly believe it was not hers; he pressed it to his lips with love and reverence, for the first time in his life fully realising the meaning of brotherhood. With that pain and that new vision his heart awoke once more, his work lay before him, his perplexity melted in a rush of love and pity, and that eager longing to help which swallows up diffidence and proves its own guide.

'Nita *mia!*' he said, his tears falling fast on the little white hand, 'do not cry like that. She is at rest—at rest, and very happy; we dare not wish her back again.'

'But I—but I have killed her!' sobbed Anita.

'No, never say that—never think it,' he cried;

'you did right to come home, quite right. It is the will of God.'

No contact with Enrico's sceptical philosophy had been able to mar that wonderful childlike faith which is one of the most beautiful characteristics of an Italian. *È volete di Dio.* The words were spoken with a grave simplicity which would have startled an Englishman. He did not pause to think of the proper thing to say, or reflect for one instant how his words would affect others, he just spoke out the perfect assurance which, in his terrible grief, had been his own refuge.

'You must know, Nita,' he resumed, as she grew more quiet, 'that I have heard all; she told me; and she died happy because she was sure you would be saved from this. You will not let her hope be vain.'

'If you would help me,' faltered Anita.

'I will—I will!' he cried eagerly. That was no time to think of details or of difficulties, he could only give her his unqualified promise. Then, when the two had discussed things a little more, it was arranged that Carlo should write a note to Merlino, and tell him that Anita would remain for a few days at the Villa Bruno.

'And, oh! write carefully,' exclaimed Nita; 'see that you do not offend him.'

Carlo wrote a cautiously worded letter, and sent it in to Naples by old Florestano, who also bore the ill news to Guido Donati and to the Ritters, and, that he might make all the more speed, was prevailed on to accept a seat in the carriage which had brought Nita that morning. }

Thus in a weary round of petty duties the time wore on, and at length night came. Carlo slept little, however, and rose the next day but ill prepared for the work before him. Nothing but the lifelong habit of making his own needs stand second to the needs of others, kept him up. With regard to the funeral there was little for him to arrange, as all was managed after the usual custom by one of the *congregazione*, the relatives not even going to the church or the grave. But he had to interview Father Cristoforo, to talk to Captain Britton, to receive Uncle Guido, who drove over from Naples at noon, and to do his best to shield Anita from reproaches, taking good care that the elder Donati should not hear one word about Comerio.

And always through the livelong day, above his grief, above the well-meant condolences of his friends, there rang in his head one unanswerable question—how to save Nita; and with that Francesca's words, 'No one but you!' In the evening, when all was over and the sad coming and going had given place to a terrible, oppressive quiet, his grief and perplexity made him turn to Enrico Ritter, with the feeling that unless he unburdened his mind to some one he should lose his senses. It was true that Francesca partly divined his trouble, but he could not discuss his difficulties with her, could not bear to unfold to her so dark a page. Sardoni, his informant, was a total stranger; Captain Britton was the last man to whom he could turn; while Uncle Guido, with his uncertain temper, and his wrath at the stain which Anita had already brought upon the family name, was little likely to give helpful counsel in this matter. Enrico, 'purely to please himself,' had hastened over to Villa Bruno, and now inevitably Carlo turned to him, and, exacting a promise of secrecy, told him everything that had happened since their last meeting.

He had chosen his confidant well. Enrico could be trusted to keep perfect silence; moreover, his sound common sense, his cool, calm, practical way of looking at things, was precisely what Carlo needed. His own brain was so overwrought, so confused with the sudden calamity which had befallen him, that he was not in the least capable of seeing any matter in its true light. And then, too, the mere relief of sharing his perplexities with another was an inexpressible comfort. Not that Enrico had many suggestions to offer; he listened for the most part in silence. But then there are times in life when the silence of a friend is the one thing for which we crave; and Carlo turned to the unspoken sympathy of the man who really cared for him when wearied with the condolences of outsiders. Guido Donati had spoken of returning the next day to discuss the future, but the really perplexing future was discussed with the German pessimist.

'There is only one thing I would advise you,

and that is, have no personal communication with Comerio,' said Enrico at length. 'I have seen him, and, into the bargain, know a good deal about him, and he's the veriest devil you can conceive. Pay him back the money, but do so through some third person.'

'I'm sure I have no wish to see him,' said Carlo, sighing. 'If only I could think of some way of getting rid of him.'

That there would be any difficulty in raising the money had not as yet occurred to Carlo. He had been extremely careless about money matters all his life; and though leading too secluded a life to be precisely extravagant, he had allowed things to drift, well content so long as he received his small annual allowance from his mother, and never troubling his head about the amount of their actual income. He knew that he was to be his uncle's heir, and to receive a very comfortable allowance from him on his marriage, therefore he left all details to his mother, took what came to him, and lived on in serene comfort. Compelled now to face the situation he was startled to find how entirely dependent he was upon his uncle; the income upon which they had lived had been derived from an annuity, and of course ceased at his mother's death; the Villa Bruno was only rented by the year, and though its furniture belonged to him it was worth but little. His only other possession was his horse, and he could not well part with that to raise the necessary money, for not only would it at once have provoked a question from his uncle, but it was indispensable to him so long as he lived in that remote country place. In the end Enrico, becoming aware of his embarrassment, said that he should ask his father to advance him the money; and as the need of a loan was quite comprehensible to Herr Ritter at such a time, he very willingly acceded to the request, and Enrico himself was charged with the disagreeable errand of conveying the money to Comerio.

This was one step in the desired direction, and one care off Carlo's mind, but his perplexity about Anita only increased, for, as each day he learnt to know her better, he was forced to own to himself how utterly unfit she was for the difficult life before her. Her beauty, her weakness, her moral cowardice, her miserable marriage, all were against her. She seemed incapable of really loving, capable only of a sort of desire to be caressed and shielded. Carlo gained a certain amount of influence with her, just because she trusted like a child to his strength, and was quite certain that he would do what he could for her; but she left everything to him, and, in those bitter days of his grief and perplexity, lived on in a placid, restful state which was almost happiness.

At length an interruption came to this state of things. One afternoon Sardoni drove over from Naples; Carlo was heartily glad to see him, and received him with a warmth which seemed to please the Englishman.

'I was afraid you would always dislike me as the bearer of ill news,' he said; 'I came partly to give you back your letter, which, of course, I have not had a chance of giving to Madame Merlino. She is still with you?'

'Yes, she is still here,' said Carlo, tearing the letter in pieces, and stifling a sigh as he remembered how different all had been when he wrote it.

'I came partly to warn you that Merlino intends soon to send for your sister,' said Sardoni; 'indeed, it is really a necessity that she should come back, for the first rehearsal is on Monday, and the theatre is to open next Thursday.'

'So soon! And as yet I have done nothing!' exclaimed Carlo.

'Are you so sure of that?' asked Sardoni, with a keen glance at him. 'You have at any rate succeeded in making Comerio your bitter enemy; and, by-the-bye, I have discovered one thing which may, perhaps, be of service to you; Comerio's engagement was for three years, but may be terminated in half that time either at Merlino's option or at his own.'

'When does the first half expire?'

'In three weeks' time,' said Sardoni.

Carlo thought for a few minutes in silence; then he said somewhat abruptly,—

'I wish you would just tell me plainly what sort of man Merlino is; I can gather but little from what my sister lets fall about him.'

'I can't draw a very pleasing picture of him,' said Sardoni, with a smile, 'for, truth to tell, there is no love lost between us. He has very little education, but that is a subject of regret to him; since his marriage he has become moral and respectable, but he is the most awful tyrant I ever had the misfortune to meet with. Of course his position tends to foster a love of power; for don't you see the manager of an operatic company is like a king, not a constitutional one, but a despot—an autocrat? Then your sister, if you will pardon my bluntness, was the very last sort of wife he ought to have had. She is afraid of him and has no notion of holding her own, and he — great brute — treats her abominably. Why don't you persuade her to try for a separation?'

'I could not be a party to that,' said Carlo, 'so long as he is faithful to her. That a man has a bad temper is no fit reason for breaking the marriage vow.'

'Those notions are old-fashioned,' said Sardoni, with a rather pitying smile.

But the smile quickly died away; for Carlo,

with a dignity indescribable, made him a little bow and dismissed the subject with a calm—
'That is very possible, signor.'

There was a world of expression, both in tone and gesture, and Sardoni saw that to argue about his suggestion would be useless.

'If you reject that idea,' he said, after a silence, 'there is only one alternative—Comerio must be got rid of. I have thrown out as many hints as I dare to Merlino, all to no purpose. To tell him the truth plainly would make him ten times more brutal to your sister, and is altogether out of the question, even if one had the right. Why, he would be a fiend incarnate! You know what Italian husbands are when once their jealousy is stirred up.'

Carlo involuntarily smiled, then, tickled by the speaker's ingenuous remark, fairly laughed.

Sardoni looked confused.

'I beg your pardon,' he said; 'but indeed I had forgotten that I was not talking to a fellow-countryman—a compliment to your accent, you see. Where did you become such a proficient?'

'Our nearest neighbours are English,' said

Carlo, not caring to explain any further, though instinctively his eyes turned towards a photograph of Francesca which stood on the mantelpiece. Sardoni's keen eyes noted this. He observed the photograph with secret admiration and drew his own conclusions.

'Then how do you propose that Comerio shall be got rid of?' said Carlo, breaking the silence. 'You do not imagine, signor, that we Italians—about whom, it appears, you are in the habit of generalising — carry stilettos and conveniently dispose of our foes by a stab?'

'There is only one way of getting rid of him,' said Sardoni. 'Merlino is always trying to cut down expenses, and with very good reason, for, as I told you before, the opera is not always a paying concern. Now, if before the agreement with Comerio is renewed you can find a baritone with as good a voice who will sing on lower terms, then I have little doubt that Merlino would settle with him and give Comerio his *congé*.'

'You must have been talking with Piale, signor?' said Carlo, conscious of a vague feeling of discomfort.

'Piale?' said Sardoni, looking puzzled; 'I do not know any one of the name.'

'Ah! then it was only an odd coincidence. But he is a well-known professor, and he has a pupil—a baritone—whom he is very anxious to bring out; he was talking to me about it only a few days ago.'

'Why, then, there is good hope for our plans,' said Sardoni. 'A beginner would expect far less than Comerio, and, if he really has a good voice and some dramatic power, no doubt Merlino would catch at him. What sort of looking fellow is he? Have you seen him? Is he presentable?'

A bright, sudden smile lit up Carlo's sad face for a minute.

'Of that I am no fit judge,' he said demurely, 'for I am the pupil in question.'

'You!' ejaculated Sardoni, in amazement. Then, recollecting his question, he began to laugh. 'Well, I have my answer in an unmistakable form. There can be no doubt that you are well fitted for the stage.'

Again his companion made that funny little Italian bow, in which there lurked so much dignity. There was just a shade of irony in his expression.

'I see the prospect does not attract you,' said Sardoni; 'yet I should fancy you might do great things on the stage, from the look of you.'

'But I hope for a very different life, signor.'

'I see. Well, I would be the last to tell you that our life is an enviable one. Some people seem to fancy that an actor's life is "all beer and skittles"—I thought so once myself, but I can tell you that's a confounded mistake.'

Carlo had never felt less inclined to discuss the merits of theatrical life; he devoutly wished that Sardoni would go; that feeling of vague discomfort grew upon him.

'Well,' he said, 'I will see if possibly Piale may know of someone else capable of taking Comerio's place; and I am greatly obliged to you, signor, for your suggestions and your help.'

Sardoni perceived that he wished to be alone, and, leaving a message of inquiry for Madame Merlino, took his departure.

But the discomfort which his presence had kept vague and undefined, broke into a clear, torturing perception when Carlo was once more alone. Over and over the words rang in his head—'No one but you!—no one but you!' He tried to stifle them, he argued with himself on the folly of the idea—he said it was impossible, Quixotic, preposterous. Finally, he hurried off to Casa Bella.

CHAPTER VIII.

PIALE SCHEMES.

'Wilt thou go forth into the friendless waste
That hast this Paradise of pleasure here?'
The Light of Asia.

THERE are some who consider that a hero must be practically immaculate, and who grumble sorely if called upon to study the life of an ordinary mortal who often stumbles when the road is rough, who shrinks from the Valley of Humiliation and takes a foolish, fleeting delight in Bypath Meadow. But if the function of all art is to picture life,—not to photograph, but to paint it,—then, without doubt, the typical hero of romance with his faultless features and his preternatural nobility must disappear for ever from the canvas; for where are these perfect beings who, in spite of cruel circumstances, never fall, who never harbour selfish thoughts—never speak hasty words?

Thank God, one meets plenty of good men,

but the best of them would certainly own that there had been times when they had felt ready to tear their tongues out in vain regret for irrevocable words—that they would give almost anything to live over again some misguided bit of their lives.

Carlo Donati was not an immaculate hero of romance, but a nineteenth-century man,—a man of flesh and blood, with a quick, ardent, sanguine temperament and strong passions. When those words which the English tourist let fall in the Neapolitan *caffè* had arrested his attention, he had been pricked at heart, and for the time vaguely disquieted. A yet deeper impression had been made upon him by his promise to his mother on her death-bed. Still, all had been vague and formless. Now, Sardoni's bald, matter-of-fact statement had plunged the sword much farther, had called up before him a plain, unmistakable way of helping Anita. The typical hero would of course have flung himself into the breach without an instant's hesitation, but Carlo did no such thing; he did not even allow his thoughts to dwell on the possibility, but just turned his back on the whole matter, tried to make Anita's visit as pleasant as might be, and sought refuge from his own sad memories in daily meetings with Francesca.

He did, however, to some extent follow Sardoni's advice, and, intrusting Piale with as much of the truth as he deemed necessary, wrote to ask him whether he knew of any singer who might be found to take Comerio's place. He also wrote to Merlino, obtaining further leave of absence for his sister, on condition that she drove in to Naples each day next week for rehearsal, and finally returned when the performances began. The days sped by rapidly enough, and on the Thursday, true to his promise, Carlo took his sister back, parting with her at the entrance to the Palazzo Forti, not without regret and apprehension. Mingled, however, with these came a sense of deep relief, for, from a selfish point of view, he could not but revel in his regained freedom: his life could never again be what it had been before Anita's return, but a sort of after-glow of the old times seemed to rise in his sky when the cloud of poor Nita's immediate presence was removed. He felt hopeful, too, for Piale had written to ask him to call at twelve o'clock, and he thought that perhaps he had found a desirable baritone.

The old Maestro received him very kindly, but soon dashed his expectations to the ground.

'I know of no one,' he said emphatically,— 'no one. You speak as if good baritones were as rife as mushrooms. And, look you, Comerio is a clever actor, and has a fine voice; you'll not easily find any one to beat him, and if you did it is unlikely enough that they would take lower terms. Besides, Merlino is extremely unpopular as a manager; only just now I had his conductor in, a capital young fellow—Marioni, and he says that they all find it almost impossible to work with him. You must give up that idea; I, at any rate, cannot help you in it.'

Carlo sighed, and fell into deep thought. He did not hear footsteps on the stairs, nor notice that some one entered the inner room, which was divided from the front one only by a curtain. But Piale heard, and abruptly changed the subject.

'You have been neglecting your voice, I fear,' he said, looking critically into his pupil's face, and grieving to see what a change trouble had wrought in it. 'Not that I blame you in the least; there are times, of course, when even music must go to the wall. Let me hear you.'

He made him work for a time at *solfeggi*, then broke into an impatient exclamation, forgetting everything but his art. 'Out of practice—shockingly out of practice,' he said, with a portentous frown, 'try this.'

He took down a copy of '*Faust*' and played the opening bars of '*Dio Possente*.' The frown and the impatient ejaculation incited Carlo, he cared intensely to please his old master, and, throwing his whole soul into the music and losing his own identity in that of Valentino, he gave an almost perfect rendering of the song.

Suddenly the curtain between the two rooms was torn back, and a black-bearded man, with swarthy face, and extremely small, dark eyes, with a restless, irritable look in them, hastened forward.

'Signor Piale, I congratulate you!' he exclaimed, 'you have produced the most promising singer of the day! No wonder you are proud of your pupil!'

He was evidently carried away by the excitement of the moment, for his face, naturally most disagreeable, was illuminated with the same glow of artistic delight which, as the song proceeded, had softened Piale's rugged features.

For a minute an observer would have noticed that the two listeners had forgotten everything but their art, while Carlo was still Valentino, not himself. There was a silence, the old Maestro looked triumphantly happy, the stranger turned his small, restless eyes on the singer, and Carlo gradually awoke to the recollection that he was not Valentino going off to the war and praying for the safety of his sister, but Anita's brother with far greater cause for anxiety, and with his hopes of assistance from Piale dashed to the ground.

All at once he came to full consciousness of the actual present, and found the stranger undisguisedly taking stock of him, looking him over from head to foot with interest and curiosity. Carlo, unaccustomed to this sort of appraising stare, felt the blood rush to his cheeks, yet it was no sense of the stranger's rudeness which aroused his strong antipathy. He looked hastily at the black-bearded visitor, looked again, angry with himself at being so much moved, then instinctively he recoiled a pace.

'The likeness is extraordinary!' exclaimed the new-comer, turning to Piale and startling him from his happy reverie.

'Likeness!' ejaculated the old musician, still half in the clouds, but dimly perceiving that sublunary affairs were somehow gone awry. 'Likeness! Not at all, signor, not at all; there's not a voice like that in all Italy.'

'I don't speak of the voice,' said the stranger, impatiently, 'but the face is like my wife's—curiously like.'

The old musician looked dismayed; he was fully awake now, art was forgotten, and a perilous bit of real life lay before him. In two strides Carlo was beside him, his face flushed, his eyes full of suppressed anger.

'Maestro,' he panted, 'what is this? what is this that you have done to me?'

'Forgive me,' said the old man, 'I am not so much to blame as you think. I did indeed invite Signor Merlino to hear you sing, but with the understanding that he should not appear. You broke faith with me, signor.'

'A thousand pardons,' said Merlino, coolly; 'but in truth your pupil ought to be pleased with the compliment. I was so carried away by his singing that I forgot all. I don't understand what all this fuss is about.'

He glanced at Carlo, who had turned away at his first words, and stood now at the window with his back to them, evidently struggling to restrain an outburst of passion. Piale looked at him, too, with compunction, but with great bewilderment. How was he to get matters set right? how disentangle himself from the confusion into which Merlino's impulsive entrance had plunged everything?

Carlo stood looking out into the busy street, but he saw nothing, was conscious of nothing but that Merlino was in the room with him—

Merlino, the cause of all his sorrow and perplexity. He had conquered by a supreme effort the first savage impulse to fly at the throat of the man who had caused his mother so much grief, but fierce anger still burnt in his heart and sent fiery blood coursing through his veins. A storm of wrathful indignation consumed him as he thought of Merlino's misdeeds; he was angry, too, with Piale, feeling naturally enough that a snare had been laid for him; and he was angry with himself because even in this moment of confusion he was aware that he had deliberately turned his back on the question now forced upon him, and that want of preparation was his own fault.

For moments of what seem to us sudden temptation are seldom really sudden. God has given us our times of preparation, and if we have wilfully neglected them the conflict is severer, or perhaps ends in defeat.

How was he now to think out the frightfully involved question at issue? How decide on the right course of action? And yet a false step might prove Nita's ruin. The anguish of that thought, and the loathing of his own selfish procrastination, calmed his anger. With an effort he yielded up his will, and therewith forgot Merlino's presence, because another presence absorbed him wholly.

He was interrupted by a touch on his arm. Piale stood beside him, with a look of deep concern on his kind old face.

'Carlo *mio*,' he said, in a low voice, 'I apologise to you, and beg your forgiveness; but since things have so fallen out, perhaps you will permit me to introduce you to Signor Merlino, who will then understand us better.'

Carlo assented, subduing the angry thoughts which yet struggled to find place in his heart.

'Signor,' said the old musician, approaching Merlino, 'there is nothing extraordinary in the likeness you observed. Permit me to introduce you to Signor Donati.'

Merlino started violently, and for a minute looked abashed, and greatly confused. Piale with much curiosity watched his pupil, who had turned from the window as he spoke, and now, with a face as pale as death, bowed gravely.

There was an awkward pause, broken presently by Carlo.

'I brought my sister to Palazzo Forti an hour ago, signor,' he said, speaking to Merlino with grave courtesy; 'I am much obliged to you for sparing her to me so long.'

The speech cost him a great deal, but he was glad that he had brought himself to make it, for he had no wish to quarrel with Nita's husband, indeed he fully recognised Merlino's rights, though unable to think patiently of the way in which he had acquired them, or the manner in which he now abused them.

'A few days' rest will doubtless have been good for Anita,' said Merlino, complacently, speaking of his wife much as he might have spoken of an over-worked horse; 'she has had hard work in America, nor can we afford now to be idle. It is a pleasure to me to make your acquaintance, signor. If I could induce you to follow your sister's example and use your great talents professionally it would give me the greatest satisfaction.'

Carlo's heart began to throb painfully. Could

it be that he was called to this? Could it be that this man—this coarse, brutal tyrant—was to prove the arbiter of his destiny? The words which a few days before he had used so emphatically to Sardoni trembled on his lips, 'I hope for a very different life.' But he managed to strangle them. Had he not offered up his will? He stood silent, waiting for guidance, hoping against hope, as is the way with poor mortals, that, after all, his own will might be done. He waited. At length Piale spoke; the words fell on him like blows.

'I have long urged upon my pupil, signor, the duty of going on the stage, for which he is admirably fitted. I am not without hope that circumstances may prompt him at length to consent. But there is as yet no vacancy in your troupe, I think, so I fear that you will not have the honour of introducing to the public both Madame Merlino and Carlo Donati.'

Carlo stood silently listening to the discussion of his fate, looking now at Piale's brown, wrinkled face, with its parchment-like skin, furrowed brow, and crown of bushy, grizzled hair, now at the disagreeable face of Merlino. He knew that when the Impresario spoke next he would say that Comerio's engagement might be terminated very shortly if he so willed; knew that Merlino was once more appraising him, observing the symmetry of his face and figure, calculating whether he would 'draw.' He felt like a slave in the market, but still he waited and held his peace.

'It shall not be my fault if I lose the honour,' said Merlino at length; 'by good luck Comerio's engagement is terminable at eighteen months if I so please; may be ended, that is, in a fortnight's time. What say you, Signor Piale? Could you have your pupil fit to fill the vacancy in so short a time as that?'

Piale was not to be daunted, though he knew well enough that the time was very short indeed for the preparation which would be necessary.

'Whether Comerio's costumes could be altered for him so soon is perhaps doubtful,' he replied proudly; 'they might or might not be ready in a fortnight's time; but my pupil will be ready— quite ready.'

'Well, I'll risk it,' said Merlino, who was a keen-eyed man of business, and knew that Carlo would prove a good speculation. 'I am prepared to offer you, signor, an engagement of three years, terminable at the end of the first year at the wish of either party. As to the salary, we shall not quarrel I think, " *Oro è, che oro vale*," let me see——'

He began to make a calculation and to discuss money matters with Piale, who, in his delight at the prospect of at length inducing his pupil to go on the stage, was ready to accede to almost any terms.

Carlo, still with that thought of the slave-market in his mind, watched the discussion like one in a dream, paying little heed to the details. It mattered nothing to him, just then, whether he received five pounds a-week or fifty; it mattered supremely that he had prayed for guidance, and that immediately after there had come to him this definite offer. He dared not refuse, he hesitated to accept. Silencing the fiends' voices which urged him at once to decline Merlino's proposal, at once to seek the selfish peace which that decision would bring, he braced himself up for a reply. The haggling at length ended, and Merlino turned to him.

'Well, Signor Donati, you hear my offer, and Signor Piale approves of the terms; it rests with you now to accept them or not. It is not for me to advise you either one way or the other; but, in my own mind, I have little doubt that, if you work well, you will be one of the first singers of the day.'

Piale's eyes shone; he could hardly contain himself, so great was his excitement. It damped his ardour to see that this glorious prospect brought no faintest gleam of pleasure to his pupil's face. He scratched his parchment-like cheek ferociously, a trick which he had when anything annoyed him or tried his patience. At length Carlo spoke:

'I am obliged to you for your offer, signor, but you will understand that it is impossible for me to accept it on the spur of the moment. The decision will affect others; I must think of them as well as of myself. I must consult those who belong to me.'

'Well, well,' said Merlino, impatiently, 'so long as you keep the matter quiet—so long as it does not come to Comerio's ears, I don't object to that; but I can't afford to be off with him till I am on with you.'

'I promise you all shall be kept quiet,' said Carlo. 'How soon must you know my decision?'

'Meet me next Wednesday at the Mercadante —or, better still, if Signor Piale will permit, at this house, and I will have the contract ready. That leaves you nearly a week, and I shall quite hope for a favourable reply. I shall, in the meantime, not breathe a word of this to my wife, who, of course, will be charmed to have you in the troupe. Good-day, signor, and let me entreat you not to throw away this opportunity. A thousand thanks, Signor Piale, for your courtesy, and pray forgive my impetuous entrance.'

He bowed himself out.

Carlo watched him as he walked down the street—watched him in a sort of stupor. When he had disappeared, his eyes turned to a heavily laden mule just coming into sight, with waving green boughs tied about its head to keep off the flies; it toiled patiently on, the lazy boy in charge hanging on to its tail with his right hand, while he devoured a great hunch of bread clasped fast in his left. Carlo watched with a sort of envy the placid calm of the sunburnt lad—that picture of lazy content contrasted so oddly with the state of his own mind. Piale soon added to the fierceness of the storm by urgent and almost piteous entreaties that he would accept Merlino's offer. With tears in his eyes, the old musician paced to and fro, passionately declaiming upon the sacred calling, and the duty of not allowing such great gifts to rust unused; and Carlo listened with the reluctant attention of one who does not wish to be persuaded. It was bad enough to fight against his own convictions; he did not want Piale's arguments to make the conflict yet more severe.

'I tell you,' urged the old man, 'that Italian opera is dying—dying for want of fit exponents. There is scarcely a man whom one cares to listen to, and it will never be kept alive by two or three *prime donne*. You might revive it, and yet you hesitate. *Corpo di Bacco!* Is it that you are unaware of your gifts? Is it that your very modesty is to prove the bane of your life and the destruction of my hopes? Listen to me—it is the plain truth I am telling you, and you well know I never flatter. For years upon years Italy has produced no great tenor, or baritone, or bass; now she has produced you; and, if you work well, you will be the first singer in Europe. Italy has produced you, and then you persist in hiding your light under a bushel! *Diavolo!* 'tis enough to try the patience of a saint!'

'Dear Maestro,' said Carlo, with a faint smile, 'what can I do more than promise to consider this offer? How can you expect me to decide all in a moment? Ah!'—a quick sigh escaped him —'Do you not see what it will involve?'

'*Hein!* What it will involve? Why, yes; I understand that it might postpone your marriage for a time. Art demands some sacrifices.'

'And what right have I to sacrifice Francesca's happiness? To a duty perhaps even that might be right, but to a dream of fame—never!' He laughed; the idea when put into words seemed to him so preposterous.

'Happiness be damned!' cried Piale, with

righteous indignation. 'I have yet to learn that Italy produced you, and England produced Miss Britton. that you might be happy. And do I not know Miss Britton? Can I for one moment dream that she would wish to hold you back? Why, by all saints, no! My dear boy, you are young—young. Believe me, a girl is always willing to wait when the good of her lover is in question. As to Captain Britton, he can't have lived all these years in Italy and yet retain his Puritan notions in all their strictness. He may object at first, but, hearing all the circumstances of the case, he will soon give way. Courage, Carlo *mio!* For a great gain, a momentary sacrifice!'

Perhaps it was that word 'momentary' which showed Carlo plainly what he had before felt dimly, that Piale knew nothing whatever about the sacrifice in question.

Much as he loved the old man, he could bear his presence no longer, but hastily took leave with a few incoherent words about 'time' and 'thinking it over.' He fled from his old singing-master as those in trouble or perplexity always do flee from glib talk. It is the one intolerable thing, as exasperating to the nineteenth-century man as the glib talk of Eliphaz, Bildad, and Zophar, was to poor Job.

'Momentary, indeed! A momentary sacrifice!' The idea made him indignant and yet pitiful. Had Piale lost his manhood in his art-life? Had he so little conception of what it was to love that he could speak thus? And then he tried to imagine to himself the fulfilment of the Maestro's wish; he had a vision of himself, old and grey-headed, enjoying the sense of his fame and his world-wide reputation, and calmly advising some other in the heyday of youth to renounce love and happiness.

It was not till he was confronted by a huge poster, in which the names of Madame Merlino and Comerio shone out conspicuously, that he once more perceived the true facts of the case. This was no question between the merits of marriage and of art-life; it was the question whether he should choose happiness for Francesca and himself, or choose the possibility of saving his sister. Life is made up of such decisions—some of them petty, some of them overwhelmingly great, but all of them momentous. We hate the thought of the choice, long to gain without losing, hope to triumph without sacrifice, strive and struggle and fret in the vain effort to break through the inexorable law that those who find their life must first lose it. Truly, 'men are not more willing to live the life of the Crucified.'

Again those words returned to Carlo's mind; they grated upon him even more than when he had first heard them spoken—perhaps because, while far from understanding them, he began vaguely to perceive their drift. He saw a dim, distasteful vision of self-renunciation; he did not see that true self-renunciation implies the peace-giving presence of One in whose service we renounce.

While he was still all confused and agitated by this inward conflict he was waylaid by Herr Ritter.

'Whither away?' exclaimed the old man, kindly. 'You are never thinking of going to Pozzuoli in this heat. Come home with me; it is long since I saw you. You are looking fagged, Carlo.'

Recollecting the obligation he was under to Enrico's father, Carlo felt that it would not do to refuse his hospitality, though, truth to tell, he had never felt less inclined for a visit to the kindly German household. He, the laughter-loving, felt that he could not endure the sound of laughter; he, the impulsive and unreflecting, had actually come to such a point that he desired nothing so much as quiet and solitude to think out this great question.

He did not get much quiet in the Ritter household, but he met with that hearty, vociferous kindness which Enrico's family knew so well how to bestow. Frau Ritter had never before been so motherly, the daughters of the house never so anxious to do what they could for him. Enrico himself was unusually silent; he watched his friend narrowly, perceiving from his face that matters must be worse rather than better since their last meeting. Possibly, however, the parting with his sister might account for the troubled expression he bore; and when, after dinner, the two friends were left alone, Enrico turned eagerly to the subject which the others had studiously avoided.

'Madame Merlino has left you, I suppose?' he began. 'She makes her first appearance to-night, I see.'

'She left this morning,' said Carlo, 'and sings to-night in *Don Giovanni.*'

'Why should you go back to the empty house? Spend the night here,' suggested Enrico.

Carlo hesitated.

'It would be my best chance of seeing Comerio,' he said, thoughtfully.

'How do you mean?'

'If I slept here and went this evening to the Mercadante.'

'*Gran Dio!* It would scarcely be an enjoyable evening for you, my friend.'

Carlo made an expressive gesture with his shoulders.

'Perhaps not, but I should see him and be able to judge better what to be at.'

'You have not heard, then, of a baritone fit to step into his shoes?'

'I have heard of one, but it is doubtful whether he will accept Merlino's offer.'

'What! Has it gone so far as that? Actually

an offer? Come, the clouds begin to disperse! Once get that scamp ousted and your troubles are over.'

Carlo was silent. In his heart he thought they would be, not over, but just begun. He had not yet told Enrico of Piale's little plot, for he knew that his friend would favour no plan likely to make him unhappy, and felt that he was not yet strong enough to stand arguments for the side on which he was already biassed.

'Well, I will stay the night since you ask me,' he said at length. 'Will you come with me to *Don Giovanni?*'

'Yes, if you are indeed bent on going. Your presence will be commented on, though. You see it is so soon after——' he broke off in confusion, adding, after a pause, 'And you see everyone will be there to-night, for Madame Merlino's first appearance has been much talked of. Your going may be misunderstood.'

'*Che sarà sarà,*' said Carlo, with a quick sigh. 'Enough, I shall go; let us say no more about it.'

CHAPTER IX.

THE OLIVE GARDEN.

> ' Though one but say, "Thy will be done,"
> He hath not lost his day
> At set of sun.' CHRISTINA ROSSETTI.

As Enrico had predicted, the Teatro Mercadante was crowded. Not only was it the opening night, but the Neapolitan world was curious to see the new *prima donna*, this girl of good birth and breeding, who had outraged all the proprieties and eloped with her singing-master. Had it not been for his inward consciousness that there was something much worse that people might ere long say of his sister, Carlo could not have endured all that he was that night fated to overhear. On every side people discussed the Merlino-Donati scandal; but though he winced under it, the dread of the future deadened the recollection of the past, the new danger eclipsed the old shame.

He sat as though in a bad dream, waiting for the curtain to rise and disclose to him the face of this enemy of his peace; so engrossed was he with this thought that he scarcely heard the overture. He wanted to meet his foe face to face, and with a sort of shudder he reflected that in a very short time it was possible that he himself might be standing on that very stage whence Leporello was now descanting upon his master's vices. A moment more and Comerio—the *Don Giovanni* of the evening—would appear. Carlo breathed hard, drew himself together, and waited through moments which seemed like hours. Curiously enough the first sight of his foe relieved him; Comerio was not at all the ideal villain; he was a small-made, supple-looking man, with very white taper hands, and a face which at that distance looked refined—much too refined for a Don Giovanni. He sang rather well, but his acting was so execrable that Carlo forgot everything in a longing desire to substitute something lifelike for the ludicrous throwing-up of hands which seemed to be Comerio's idea of dramatic art. Never once was it possible to think of him as anything but Comerio the baritone; he walked through his part and threw about his arms very freely, that was all. And yet his complete failure as an actor was in Carlo's favour. He wanted to study the man, not to enjoy the opera, and since Comerio had no notion of throwing himself into his part, the opera was as good a time to study his own character as any other.

For a while all went well. The pretty scene in which Zerlina made her first appearance amid the crowd of merry peasants could not have been better chosen for Anita's *début*. She looked so charming, and sang so well, that she won all hearts, and even Carlo felt a thrill of pride and pleasure as he listened to her sweet, bird-like notes in the duet with Masetto, a part which was well filled by Merlino himself.

But his pleasure was of short duration. All his miserable apprehension returned the instant Comerio was on the stage again. To see him making love to Anita was more than he could endure.

Next day the newspapers were warm in their praise as to the acting in the scenes between

Don Giovanni and Zerlina; but Carlo knew that this was just the one part of the opera in which there had been no attempt at acting.

The music was poisoned to him that night, and he could hardly endure the repetition of '*La ci darem*,' which roused the audience to enthusiasm. He never spoke once to Enrico, who for his part could only speculate as to his friend's feelings, for Carlo showed no other sign of agitation than a slightly heightened colour, sat out the opera, and greeted two or three friends whom they encountered afterwards quite in his usual manner. Only one thing seemed ominous, because it was unnatural, and that was his silence. It grew so burdensome as they walked home that at last Enrico broke the ice with an outspoken question, 'Well, what do you think of him?'

'I don't know—I can hardly tell—my head aches too much,' said Carlo, in a voice which betrayed so much suffering that his friend ventured no more inquiries, and was glad enough when they reached home. 'I shall think things out better to-morrow,' were his last words that night. But when the morning came he was incapable of thinking at all, and could only lie still and endure the worst headache he had ever had in his life, while, as though to torture him yet more, '*La ci darem*' rang perpetually in his ears.

On the Saturday he awoke to the consciousness that the pain was over, that his brain was clear once more, and that he must no longer postpone the decision upon which so much depended. But Frau Ritter absolutely refused to allow him to go home till the heat of the day was over; and it was not until late that he managed to escape from his kindly nurses, and, taking a boat at the Piliero, made his way home. He felt much shaken by all that he had been through, and would fain have given himself up to the refreshment of the sweet June evening, turning his back on the threatening future, and getting what pleasure he could from the beautiful bay which was so familiar and so dear to him. But something warned him that now was his time, that he was not likely again to have such uninterrupted quiet.

Resolutely he went over in his mind all that there was to be said on either side of the question. What course would Captain Britton take? Would he not justly complain of an arrangement which must indefinitely postpone his daughter's marriage? Would he not be wrathful at his choice of such a profession? And how was he to explain to him that choice without altogether betraying Nita's story? Again, there was the profession itself. Piale thought only of the reputation he would some day gain, but Carlo, not unnaturally, thought of the reputation he would lose. He knew quite well how his friends would regard his choice: he could imagine the expression of Uncle Guido's face as he exclaimed, 'What! a Donati turn actor?'

And then there was Francesca. His breast heaved, his eyes grew dim; had it not been for the presence of the boatman he would have given way and sobbed aloud. And yet Piale was right as far as that went. Once convinced that he might really save Nita, Francesca would be the first to bid him go; once sure that he was doing what he thought right, she would bid him

God-speed and bear the pain like a little heroine.

With him rested the real difficulty, the terrible decision. Was he to give her this pain to bear?

'There will be stormy weather to-night, signor,' said the boatman, turning round in his seat to glance out seawards as they rounded Posilipo.

This remark diverted Carlo's thoughts for a moment. The sea was like glass, far away in the distance he could see a yacht lying becalmed, her beautiful white sails flapping idly as she rolled.

The sunset was just over, and already the brief twilight was fading away, the summer night beginning, and after the sultry, almost breathless day, a cool wind was springing up; on the horizon could be seen the dark line which showed that a change was coming, and that the time of calm inaction was over.

Was it not like his life? He had had his days of ease, his smooth, uneventful days, with nothing to mar the tranquil happiness. Then there had arisen the dark foreboding of coming trouble, and now the storm had broken. Was he to choose this life of perpetual storm? Or might he not seek the tranquil haven where he longed to be? Must he indeed go forth into a world so uncongenial?—into a strife so distasteful?

He was not indolent by nature, he was not selfish; but he had, in a marked degree, that Italian hatred of storm and struggle which to a northern nature is so incomprehensible. To go out into a life of perpetual temptation,—a life likely to be full of provocations to the temper, this was harder to him than to most men, for he dreaded nothing so much as losing his self-control. What if he should accept this offer, go forth as Nita's preserver, and then fail himself? In that case, indeed, all would have been lost, honour included. He could not risk all this for a mere hope, a mere chance. It could not surely be expected of a man that he should give up his home, his prospects of marriage, his profession, everything that he cared for, all for the sake of saving one woman? No, it certainly could not be expected! Why, the world would laugh at such a notion. Had any other man put such a case to him, he, too, would have smiled at it, and called the propounder of such folly a mere Quixote. How foolish the old boatman would think him if he steered this frail little boat out into the troubled waters yonder instead of making all speed to guide it to the shore!

He shivered slightly, threw his cloak across his chest, and, for the sake of a change of thought, began to abuse old Frau Ritter for having delayed his return so long, and in her dread of sunshine brought him in for the risk of malaria. But above it all floated the perverse voice which would not leave him unmolested: 'Men are not more willing to live the life of the Crucified.' He left off abusing Frau Ritter, and began to hum a song, but naturally enough chanced to begin with an air from *Don Giovanni*. The voice he longed to drown spoke more and more clearly. Well, *Don Giovanni* was poisoned for him, he must eschew it in future. And forthwith he strove to drive the unpleasant thoughts connected with it from his mind with the first snatch of song which came to his head.

Out into the summer night rang the noble impassioned address of Valentino to Mephistopheles:

'*La croce dai demoni tuoi ci guarda!*'

The scene in the opera rose vividly before him, the soldier, with his cross-handled sword uplifted, boldly confronting the devil who so lately had worsted him, but who now shrank back helpless and trembling. Good heavens! and he had sought to drown the voice of God in his heart by those very words, had sought to drive back the good and to give place to the evil.

A horror of great darkness fell upon him. It was the crisis of his whole life. Afterwards, when he recalled the past anguish, he recalled with it those sombre surroundings, the purple waters, the great dark cloud drawing nearer and nearer, the hopeless gloom of the night broken only by the light on Cape Miseno and the red light on the side of the yacht. Not a sound was to be heard save the splashing of the oars, and now and then a sort of hoarse shout in the distance, probably the yacht's captain giving orders to his crew; but to Carlo the silence was tumult. He was sailor enough to know that in a few minutes the storm would be upon them. That mattered little, for they were close to the shore; it was the tumult in his own heart which absorbed him.

Vaguely, and as if from a great distance, he heard the boatmen giving thanks to San Gennaro that they were safely in before the squall, he had indistinct recollections of paying the man a double fare and bidding him seek shelter for the night at Florestano's hut, then of plunging wildly on through the darkness, across the beach, up the hill among the dusky vines, his pain increased by a consciousness that when he had last trodden that path it had been with Francesca. Was it to be thus with his life? Must he content himself with a memory of the briefest snatch of happiness ever given to man, and toil on through long, solitary years over the rough and stony paths of publicity? It was impossible,—impossible! He rushed on yet faster, as though by rapid motion he could escape from the tyranny of an idea.

Just as he reached the olive-garden the storm

suddenly broke. The wind raged over the land, tossing the trees wildly to and fro; the rain came down in torrents, the lightning cast its angry gleam across the heaving sea, and the swaying boughs, and the wet, shining shore. Carlo threw himself down on the ground, beneath the thickest of the olive-trees, seeking at once shelter from the outward storm and help in the inward struggle. He would no longer flee from the voice that had haunted him; he would listen to it—would try to understand it. What *was* the life of the Crucified?

All his soul went into the question, and the confusion within him seemed to lessen as he waited for the answer, which framed itself to him amid the raging of the wind and the dull roar of the thunder, something after this fashion.

The life of the Crucified was lived by One who delighted to do God's will. He did not exclude pleasure, or morbidly delight in pain; it was just that He did not think about pleasing Himself at all. He took the bitter and the sweet as they were sent, and delighted in them because He knew the Sender who sought only the good of all men. This is the life of the Crucified. You think happiness is to please yourself;—it is not that at all, it is to delight in doing His will.

'Lord,' he sobbed, 'I am not willing—it is true—I am not willing to live Thy life. Save me from my selfishness! "By Thine agony and bloody sweat, by Thy cross and passion, Good Lord, deliver me."'

He repeated the familiar words again and again, hardly conscious of what he was saying, yet in his anguish finding them a sort of relief. And, presently, either the words or his own surroundings brought to his mind what the greatest of modern atheists once termed, with an involuntary softening of the voice, 'That terrible garden-scene.' There had been a struggle—an agony—for the Son of God Himself. He, too, knew what it cost deliberately to take the course which must bring bitter grief to those who loved Him. He, too, knew how human nature shrank from isolation, from misconception. Every temptation now assailing him had also assailed the Son who learned obedience by the things which He suffered,

And just as a child will for very awe forget its little grief when brought face to face with the great grief of its parents, so Carlo lost sight for a time of his own pain, that past scene becoming far more real to him than the bitter present. The tears wrung from him first by his own anguish fell now for another.

'Lord,' he sobbed, 'it cannot be that I am willing that Thou shouldst be crucified afresh — put to open shame—while I live here in this paradise! Anything rather than that! Lord, choose for me what Thou wilt. My spirit is willing, but my flesh is weak. "By Thine agony and bloody sweat, by Thy cross and passion, Good Lord, deliver me."'

An hour later the brief Mediterranean storm was over, the stars were shining, the yacht was on her course once more, her white sails spread to catch the softened breeze.

Then Carlo rose to his feet and went on his way.

CHAPTER X.

THE 'PILGRIM.'

'Joy, so true and tender,
Dare you not abide?
Will you spread your pinions?
Must you leave our side?
—Nay; an Angel's shining grace
Waits to fill your place!'
A. A. PROCTER.

'VERY odd of Carlo not to come in to-day,' remarked Captain Britton from the depths of his easy chair. 'I suppose the heat was too much for him. Have you heard from him, Fran?'

'I had a little note from him yesterday, father, only to say that he wasn't well and that the Ritters insisted on keeping him, but that he would be sure to be at home again on Saturday. I daresay Frau Ritter made him stay; it was so sultry, you know, and since Herr Ritter's illness she is always in terror of sunstrokes.'

'Well, one thing is, this thunder-storm will clear the air,' said the Captain, rubbing his large hands together contentedly. 'If I could be sure your uncle was safely in port, I should feel more comfortable, though. What did I do with his letter? Ah, here it is! "The yacht is to leave Leghorn on Wednesday," he says. They certainly ought to be at Naples by this time.'

'I looked out for the *Pilgrim* yesterday,' said Francesca, 'but to-day I forgot all about it. How I wish Clare and the girls were coming too; it was very benighted of them to like a stupid visit to the North Cape better than a cruise in the Mediterranean.'

'No accounting for tastes,' said the Captain, smiling. 'If it were not for this engagement of yours, I should feel sorely tempted to get your uncle to give me a berth. There is nothing, after all, like the sea. You smile, Fran. Why, bless your dear little heart! I wasn't wishing things otherwise with you and Carlo. On the contrary, I think the sooner you are married and settled the better for both of you. He has looked sadly worn and out of spirits lately, poor fellow!'

'There has been so much to trouble him,' said Francesca, with a sigh.

'Ay, and he is unfit to be left all alone in that dreary house. Really, I don't see why there should be any more delay. Now that he has got rid of that sister of his, why shouldn't you be married quietly and have done with it? No disrespect to the mother in that, poor soul! Why it is the thing of all others she would have wished. I tell you what, Fran, here is such a chance as is never likely to come again. Your uncle is unexpectedly coming out here, he is sure to give at least a week to Naples—why should we not have your wedding while he is here? Upon my word!'—he rubbed his hands with greater satisfaction than before—'that's the happiest notion that has come to me for a long time, Fran. You and Carlo shall be packed off on your honeymoon, Sibyl and I will console ourselves with a cruise in the *Pilgrim*, and we'll all forget that provoking Madame Merlino, who has made such a storm in a tea-cup.'

Francesca blushed vividly.

'If you really think — if Carlo ——,' she broke off in confusion.

Captain Britton patted her head caressingly

'Why, of course, my love, of course I would take good care that Carlo thought the suggestion his own. To prolong the engagement would be bad for both of you. Nothing in the world more trying than long engagements. Not that you are to think I am in any hurry to get rid of you; but, after all, we shall scarcely be separated, and an engagement is somehow neither one thing nor the other. I should like to see you married, my dear; this sad affair of poor Carlo's has been an annoyance to me—such things are unsettling, they interrupt the steady routine of daily life. I confess I shall be glad to go away for a time with your uncle, and then, later on, to come back and begin our ordinary life once more.'

Francesca felt like a cat rubbed the wrong way, but knowing that the rubber meant it all very kindly she bore it with composure.

'A cruise in the *Pilgrim* would be the best possible change for you,' she said, laughing lightly, though not altogether without an effort. 'I shall go and see if she is anywhere to be seen; and really, since you are in such a hurry to be off, I shall have to think about my wedding-dress.'

Glad to put an end to the conversation, she crossed the room, threw open the window, and stepped out into the *loggia*. The night was deliciously fresh after the storm; she felt an inexpressible sense of freedom and relief as she closed the window behind her, and drank in deep draughts of the cool, moist air. Though her father's words had grated upon her, there was, nevertheless, a certain amount of truth in them which she could not but recognise. She, too, had that longing to go away, to escape from the scene of all the trouble and sorrow which had lately invaded their home. It would be like escaping from the hot, lamplit drawing-room into this cool out-of-doors. And then, perhaps Carlo would begin to be himself again. Surely, though she had not liked the way in which the idea was expressed, the idea itself was a good one. They would go away,—right away from Naples,—away from the region of theatres,—away from all that could recall Carlo's loss, and she would comfort him. Then, later on, they would induce Merlino to let Anita come to them; she should stay with them at the Villa Bruno, should be made perfectly happy, should have all kinds of little English comforts which would be new and delightful to her after her wandering life. And so her troubles should somehow conveniently disappear, and she should find that their home was her home. If her trouble was connected with money, as Francesca fancied, why then Carlo would somehow manage to clear off her debts, and she, too, should start life afresh, and they would all live happily ever after. So she dreamed in her girlish fashion, knowing nothing of the real state of the case, only fully convinced that this dreary state of things could not last for ever, that somehow it would all come right in the end like the books. And in that belief no doubt she was right; wrong only in this, that 'coming right in the end' meant to her coming right in these threescore years and ten.

To be married, perhaps, next week! How calmly her father had suggested the idea, and how her heart throbbed as she recalled his words! She would lay aside her mourning for that one day, would be dressed, spite of the sadness which had heralded in her marriage, 'as a bride adorned for her husband;' and therewith she began, after the manner of girls, to picture the dress to herself; it should be long and white and shining; and as for orange-blossom, why there was no lack of that in the garden, always supposing this heavy rain had not dashed it. Thinking of the orange-blossom, she turned from those inward visions and looked down into the dusky mass of trees and shrubs below, starting a little at sight of someone approaching, but quickly recognising her lover.

'Carlo! why, Carlo! is it really you?' she exclaimed, an ecstasy of happiness in her voice, for she had not in the least expected him.

He looked up. She was leaning on the rail of the *loggia* among the climbing roses, her eyes bright with joy, her sweet face a little flushed, her white neck and arms gleaming through the black lace of her dress. He trembled from head to foot. It was too late now to tell her all—and had he strength to meet her? Would it not be better just to kiss that hand resting on the white balustrade, and excuse himself for the evening? But Francesca, who had never since her betrothal been so long parted from her lover, turned and flew down the steps to meet him.

'Oh, I had quite given you up, darling!' she cried. 'And are you really well again — quite well?'

A terrible pang rent his heart, but he trembled no more; all the man in him rose up to meet this sore trial.

'Quite well, *carina*; only wet through, and not fit to touch you,' he said; and by an impulse which he could hardly have explained he checked the hands which were stealing round his neck, drew them down, and held them fast in his while he bent forward and kissed her.

A shade passed over her face. Why did he stop to think about his wet clothes? What lover ever deigned to bestow a thought on such prudent considerations?

He read her thoughts in a glance, and therewith saw a vision of the future—the shadow deepening on that dear face, the eyes dim with tears, the brow contracted with pain. To hide his agony from her he let his head droop forward, resting his burning forehead on her shoulder.

'I have been so dreadfully anxious, Carlino,' she said. 'And, oh! it is so beautiful to have you back again!'

He did not speak, only his cold hands held hers more tightly; his face was hidden on her breast. But, though he could hide from her the sight of his anguish, he could not deceive her; she knew intuitively that it was no physical pain which made a man like Carlo bow his head like one overwhelmed. It must surely be that he was thinking of his mother—and it must have been terribly dreary coming back from Naples that stormy evening—coming home for the first time to the empty house.

'My own dear one,' she said, all the deep tenderness in her heart stealing into her voice, 'you'll not shut me out from your sorrow. What is yours is mine, Carlino. I was so happy when I saw you, I forgot what a sad home-coming it must be. But, darling, it wasn't that I forgot her, for I, too, loved her.'

'Pray that I may keep my promise to her,' he whispered. 'Pray! pray!'

There was a silence. The tears welled up in

Francesca's eyes, not because she understood his sorrow, but because the sorrow was his, and because she loved him. She prayed obediently like a little child. After a while he raised his head, looked for a moment into her eyes, then pressed his lips to hers in a long, lingering kiss.

'Dear love,' he said, gently, ' we will keep our Whitsuntide together.'

He watched her up the marble steps, then turned away, walking home through the wet garden paths. And even in his great sadness he could not but smile faintly as he reflected what Piale's feelings would be could he now see him, cold, and weary, and wet to the skin. ' The singer keeps his shop in his throat,' he said to himself, with a pathetic little effort to persuade himself that he was now quite accustomed to the idea. ' I must not indulge any more in evening storms.'

The next day was Whitsunday. Carlo, as usual, drove in to Naples with the Brittons, and was very glad that the great excitement of ' Uncle George's ' probable arrival excluded all other topics of conversation. It lasted throughout the drive, and, indeed, engrossed Captain

Britton's thoughts so much during church-time that he was glad to effect his escape with Sibyl after the sermon, leaving Carlo and Francesca to the second service, while he hastened to make inquiries as to the *Pilgrim*.

To his surprise and delight, he was greeted just outside the church by his brother.

Sibyl, who had very vague recollections of her uncle, studied him with a child's keen criticism.

'He is like papa,' she reflected, 'but smaller and finer; his beard is beautiful, and white and curly, like a Father Christmas; he laughs with his eyes. I like him.'

Having satisfied herself on this point, she began to listen to the conversation.

'Yes, we got in early this morning,' her uncle was saying. 'We had very light winds all the way from Leghorn—in fact, yesterday we were becalmed, but after the squall we got on better. What a paradise you live in, to be sure! Ah, is this your little one? Why, Sibyl, you have grown out of all knowledge! And what have you done with Francesca?'

'Francesca will be here directly,' replied the Captain. 'We may as well wait for her, if you are not in a hurry. By the bye, George, I think you have not heard that she is to be married shortly.'

'What high and mighty nobleman has been so happy as to meet with your approval?' said Mr. Britton, well aware of his brother's weakness for titles, and convinced by his beaming face that the marriage was desirable in his eyes.

'A young Italian neighbour of ours, Signor Donati; not a noble at all, but of a good old family, and likely to do well at the Neapolitan Bar. Oh, I am thoroughly pleased with the affair—thoroughly pleased, and Donati is heir to a rich old uncle, so it is satisfactory in every way.'

'I hope he is good enough for dear little Fran,' said Mr. Britton, drily. Somehow the notion of his pretty niece marrying the first foreigner who proposed for her did not please him.

'Well, as to that, I doubt if there is anyone in the world quite good enough for her,' said Captain Britton, rubbing his hands, but slightly

embarrassed by the presence of his Prayer-book.
'You will like Donati, though, I am sure of that.
He is a fine fellow. Just now, poor boy, he is in
great trouble—lost his mother quite suddenly,
and, of course, he's dreadfully cut up. In fact, I
think the only thing will be to hasten on the
marriage, and get him right away from the place
for a bit. Ah, here they come! that's right!'
and he hurried forward lest Sibyl should fore-
stall him as news-bearer.

Mr. Britton glanced quickly at Francesca's
fiancé, and felt his insular prejudice melting
away. A more beautiful face he had never seen.
Something of its serenity vanished, however, as
Captain Britton approached,—a sort of shade
passed over the forehead, and he evidently came
back to the present with an effort. The Captain
brought him forward, and introduced him in his
usual rather boisterous and patronising way.
Mr. Britton was all the more struck by the grace
and dignity of the Italian, and he held out his
hand cordially.

'I have been hearing of you, Signor Donati,'
he said, pleasantly. 'You must let me congratu-

late you, for, indeed, I think you are a very happy man.'

The Italian smiled, surely the saddest smile ever seen, as he bowed his acknowledgments. Mr. Britton was startled and perplexed, but Francesca's happy face reassured him, and had not the Captain said that his future son-in-law was in trouble?

'I want you all to come and spend the day on my yacht,' he said, turning to his brother. 'The gig is waiting down by the Arsenal. Come! you must really take compassion on my solitude. Signor Donati, I hope you'll put up with that barbarous custom, an early dinner; but the fact is, our cook's cuddy is so near the men's quarters that if I dine late the poor fellows are half-grilled at night.'

After a little more discussion, they all set off for the Arsenal, where the 'gig,' a term which had baffled Carlo altogether, resolved itself into a four-oared boat, manned by trim-looking English sailors, who bore the name of the *Pilgrim* in red letters across their blue jerseys, and in gold letters round their hats. Mr. Britton took his place in the stern, insisting that his brother must sit beside Sibyl to trim the boat, and, having thus managed that the lovers should be side by side, gave the word to start. Sibyl gave a cry of delight as the golden-brown oars were promptly raised in the air and simultaneously lowered into the water.

'Oh, Uncle George!' she cried, 'how happy you must be with this dear little boat always waiting for you, and men to do so beautifully just what you say!'

'Ah!' said Mr. Britton, laughing. 'Wait till you are on board the *Pilgrim!* I see,' he added, turning to Carlo and Francesca, 'that you two have already taught this little one to understand the proud sense of possession.'

Francesca smiled and blushed. Carlo appeared to be engrossed with a vessel which they were passing, the huge *Duilio*, then not quite completed.

'I suppose,' he said, turning back with a bright smile which veiled the pain at his heart, 'I suppose there is no need to introduce you to our monster vessel, you probably know much more about her than we do.'

The shipbuilder was not above appreciating the compliment thus delicately conveyed, and Francesca looked up at the unwieldy form with its dull red colour and its six funnels, and tried to seem interested in the discussion which arose upon its merits among the men; its only merit to her was that it seemed to be interesting Carlo and taking him out of himself. The *Pilgrim*, a pretty, schooner-rigged yacht, of about 150 tons, was anchored off the Military Mole, and, like all the vessels in harbour, was gaily dressed with flags in honour of the *festa*. A somewhat smaller yacht was anchored close by.

'They tell me our neighbour the *Aida* belongs to an Italian Count or Duke, or something of the sort,' said Mr. Britton. 'What was the name, Oxenberry; do you recollect?'

'Count Carossa, I believe, sir,' said the coxswain.

'Count Carossa!' said Captain Britton, with a beaming face. 'The name seems familiar to me. A friend of yours, perhaps, Carlo?'

'No, sir; I have never even met him,' said Carlo, repressively.

'But the name is familiar to you, surely?'

'It is certainly a well-known name,' said Carlo, still in the same tone.

Mr. Britton was a little puzzled, he could not make out whether the Italian knew of something not to the credit of Count Carossa, or whether his tone merely implied a great distaste of the Captain's love of the aristocracy.

By this time they were alongside the yacht, and the Captain, forgetting all about the Count, began to admire his brother's latest toy.

'A very pretty little vessel indeed, George! I confess I envy you. Sibyl, what do you say? Shall we not sell the villa and live afloat? Now, Carlo, don't forget to take your hat off to the deck, it's a mortal insult to forget that!'

Carlo laughed; just for a little time he forgot his cares, and his first thought, as he glanced round the deck, with its exquisitely smooth and white boards, its shining brass work, its cunningly arranged skylights and companions, was this:—

'A yacht is the last place in the world for private conversations. One more day of freedom! One more day's peace of mind for my darling!'

As for Sibyl, she was wild with happiness, now watching the gig as it was hauled up, now trotting off hand in hand with the coxswain to the forecastle, looking with longing eyes at the rope ladders, and chattering without intermission.

It was not without difficulty that Francesca bore her off to be washed and brushed before dinner, and had it not been for the fascinations of the shifting table in the saloon, she would hardly have been induced to stay down below for so dull a duty as eating.

'Uncle George,' she said, leaning forward in her quaint way, 'it would have been nice to come on board the *Pilgrim* any day, but being Sunday it's just perfect.'

'Eh—how's that?' said Mr. Britton. 'The better the day the better the deed, is that your idea?'

'No; but don't you see on weekdays we can have games—different games every day, if we like, but Sundays are always—always the same. Now this makes such a beautiful difference. I am glad you asked us on Sunday!'

Carlo, to whom the rules of the English Sunday had always been incomprehensible, could not repress an amused smile, but he wisely avoided taking part in the discussion which ensued on modern Sabbatarianism, being, of course, ready enough to speak out his own opinion if it were asked, but not feeling bound to volunteer it. The argument was at last interrupted by the entrance of the steward.

'A boat has just come across from the *Aida*, sir, with Count Carossa's card, but the Captain can't make out what the men say, all of them being Italians.'

Carlo at once offered to act as interpreter, and ran up on deck, returning with the message, which he delivered with an impartial face.

'Count Carossa presents his compliments to the owner of the *Pilgrim*, and it would give him much pleasure to make his acquaintance. If quite convenient to Mr. Britton, the Count will call upon him in the afternoon.'

'Very happy to see him, I'm sure,' said Mr.

Britton, who was the soul of hospitality. 'Perhaps, Signor Donati, you would be so good as to frame a polite message for me and deliver it to the messenger; or stay, I'll write it on my card.'

This done, they all adjourned to the deck, where, before long, they were joined by Count Carossa, a fine-looking man of two or three-and-thirty, to whom Captain Britton took very kindly. There was much amusing discussion as to the merits of the two yachts, then of Mr. Britton's homeward route, during which the Count discovered that Francesca and her father were living in the neighbourhood, and did his best to push the acquaintance, eliciting very easily an invitation to dinner on the following Wednesday.

Carlo, after the Count's arrival, had kept sedulously in the background, and had said but little. Happening to glance at him once Mr. Britton was struck by the strange expression of his face. He hastily turned his eyes towards Francesca; she was smiling in answer to some polite nothing addressed to her by the Count.

'I believe that fellow Donati is jealous!' he

thought to himself. 'My poor little Fran, you are altogether too good to be left to the tender mercies of an Italian husband. I wonder if the marriage is, after all, so advisable as they seem to think.'

Afterwards, when the Count was gone, he said, casually, to Carlo,—

'By the way, Signor Donati, I suppose this Count Carossa is a decent sort of fellow; you don't know anything against him, do you?'

'Nothing whatever, sir,' said Carlo, emphatically,—'nothing whatever. I only know that he is very rich, and that he leads a wandering life; I have often heard people wonder why in the world he does not settle down.'

'Then he is unmarried?'

'Yes, he is unmarried.'

At that moment Sibyl ran up to beg Carlo to look at 'some dear little tortoises in the dinghy.' Mr. Britton nodded to himself with the air of one who has surmised rightly.

'Just as I thought,' he muttered, 'as jealous as he can be.'

The afternoon was spent in rambling about

Naples, showing Uncle George as many lions as he cared to see; then they returned to the yacht to that curious English meal called 'tea,'—a new experience to Carlo, and it was arranged that they should drive home in the cool of the evening, taking Mr. Britton with them.

'It has been such a delightful day,' said Francesca; 'I think I agree with Sibyl that being a Sunday it has been all the nicer.'

The lovers were standing near the wheel in the dim starlight; perhaps Carlo was glad that the light was no clearer.

'See,' he said, 'there is Venus just setting; not there; look, out yonder behind St. Elmo.'

Francesca was just in time to see the last of the planet; after it was set, the Castle on its lofty height seemed to stand out more darkly against the evening sky. The harbour was very quiet, but from the shore came sounds of laughter and merriment, a confused roar of many voices, and now and then in the distance a line or two of Garibaldi's hymn floating on the wind.

'How still and peaceful we are out here!' said Francesca, 'and how noisy and horrid it seems in Naples. Why does a Babel like that always sound so wicked, I wonder? It makes me think of Vanity Fair in the *Pilgrim's Progress.*'

'And yet through all the uproar we can make out Garibaldi's hymn,' said Carlo.

'Ah,' she said, laughing, 'I know you would like to be in the thick of it all, fighting against the evil as your father and grandfather fought in their day. Oh, Carlino, what a good thing for me that there are no battles now!'

'Yet in a good cause you would not have hindered me, I think, *carina?* Tell me,' his lips trembled,—' tell me, had we lived then would you have begged me to stay at home?'

'No, Carlo *mio*,' she said, raising her sweet eyes to his; 'I would have told you to go and help your country; I wouldn't have cried till you were out of sight.'

They were interrupted by a summons to get into the gig, and the four trim-looking sailors rowed them swiftly across the quiet harbour, the only sound being an occasional ' *Qui va la?*' from the watchman on board one of the anchored vessels, and a ringing reply from the coxswain of 'Yacht's boat.'

'The peace of my life is over,' thought Carlo, as he glanced back across the quiet waters to the *Pilgrim* with her golden harbour light; 'now for Vanity Fair.'

CHAPTER XI.

A FIRST ENCOUNTER.

'Blest, too, is he who can divine
 Where real right doth lie,
And dares to take the side that seems
 Wrong to man's blindfold eye.

Then learn to scorn the praise of men,
 And learn to lose with God;
For Jesus won the world through shame,
 And beckons thee His road.'   FABER.

'I HAVE something to say to you, *carina;* let us linger behind the others; there is no hotter place on earth than these streets of Pompeii, and I think we know them well enough.'

The whole party had driven over early on the Monday morning to show Mr. Britton the more recent excavations; he had been to Pompeii before, but many years ago.

To Carlo and Francesca, however, those old grey streets and ruined temples were perfectly familiar, and Francesca was not sorry to follow out Carlo's suggestion, and despatched Sibyl to tell the others that they would wait in the Temple of Venus till their return.

'At which message you may be sure Uncle George will laugh,' she said. 'Had we been wise in our generation, Carlo, we should have chosen the Temple of Isis, but then this is my favourite, and, after all, we are proof against teasing now.'

Carlo smiled sadly, as he looked across the beautiful expanse of country. On one side, beyond the ruined streets, lay the verdant *Campagna* bounded by Vesuvius and Somma; on the other, was a yet more lovely view of sea and mountains, with the white houses of Castellamare gleaming in the sunshine.

'We have not chosen a very shady place,' said Francesca. 'But, see, there is just a little patch of shadow down there. Let us come.'

'Do you know what that is?' said Carlo, repressing a shudder.

'Why, yes, to be sure,' she replied gaily; 'it's the altar of sacrifice. How fond Clare used to be of poking about in here—don't you remember? I wish she had come with Uncle George.'

'And I, too; I would have given anything to have had her here—for your sake, *carina*.'

There was something so unusual in his tone that Francesca looked up quickly.

'Carlo *mio*, you frighten me! What do you mean? Don't lean on the altar like that! Come and sit down on this step by me in the shade. Why do you wish Clare here for my sake? What do I really want with any one now that I have you?'

'But if, as we were saying last night, there was a battle to fight and I had to leave you?'

'Carlino! what do you mean? Surely there is not going to be a revolution—a war?'

'Oh, no, it is much tamer than that,' he said, with a slightly bitter smile. Then, a sudden light illumining his face, he put his arm round her and held her closely.

'My dear one,' he said, speaking rapidly and with great earnestness,—' my own true love, you gave me fresh courage last night by your words. *Carina*, there are other wars than those between nations; there is the great war in which you and I have vowed our service; you would not wish me, I know, to prove coward in that—to be a deserter. I must tell you, in plain words, the actual case, even though it is hard to do it,—even though I would give the world to keep all knowledge of such evil from you. Francesca, do you know what killed my mother? I will tell you. It was the knowledge that Anita was living in hourly peril of proving unfaithful to her husband! He—that one who would ruin her—that one who dares to call his foul passion by the name of love, is actually a member of Merlino's company. Merlino himself suspects nothing, if he did he would half kill Anita. I have thought of every possible plan for getting rid of this villain without betraying my sister; but, darling, there is only one way that will answer, and it is this: to get rid of this man—this baritone—I must take his place myself.'

'You must offer,' said Francesca, faintly; 'but perhaps Signor Merlino will not accept you.'

'The post has already been offered to me by

Merlino, and on Wednesday, Francesca *mia*, I must let him know whether I accept his offer or not.'

'Ah!'

She locked her hands together convulsively, but only that one sob of intense, intolerable pain escaped her.

There was silence—a silence so deep that the distant sounds of the workmen busy over the excavations seemed quite near. A little lizard darted across the pavement close to their feet, and plunged into the maidenhair that fringed the altar.

Francesca opened her eyes.

'My love! my love!' she cried, 'don't look like that! See, Carlo *mio*, I am going to keep my word. I will say, like the wives in the old days, "Go and help," and I'll not cry; I promise you I'll not cry. And yet—yet—oh! how can I help it when you set me so bad an example?'

With a stifled sob she broke off and hid her face on his breast. The sight of her suffering had unnerved him, but quickly he regained that strange self-mastery which was all the more remarkable because it was combined with an ardent, emotional, highly-strung temperament.

'You are helping me to keep my word,' he said, drawing her yet closer to him. 'As a child I promised my father on his death-bed that I would shield Nita, and my mother's last entreaty you heard.'

'Do I help you?' she said, eagerly; 'do I really help? Then I am no longer unhappy. It was the thought of your going quite away where I could do nothing—*nothing* for you—it was that broke my heart. If, even away, I can help you—if even in this we can work together—then I can bear it.'

'Your father,' he said, hesitatingly, 'I must tell him at once,—and, *carina*, he will not see things in the light you see them.'

'He will not approve of your going on the stage,' said Francesca. 'He will be vexed and annoyed, but he cannot help seeing that it is the only thing to be done.'

Carlo made a faint gesture of dissent. The

last sentence was so like Francesca, so unlike the Captain.

'He will most naturally wish that I had never spoken to you. Indeed, I myself could almost wish it, darling; for what have I brought you but trouble, and grief, and the shadow of a disgrace?'

'You have brought me yourself, Carlino,' she said, with a sweet mirthfulness in look and tone; 'you don't seem to think much of the gift, it is true.'

'And yet if I had kept silence a week longer all would have been different. I should have gone off with Merlino's company and there would have been no discussion and remonstrance; I should not have vexed your father—should not have felt that I had spoiled your life. You would have been free, and the pain would have been mine alone.'

'Why, you vain boy!' she exclaimed, half laughing, half crying, 'do you think it was that tale you told me in the Belvedere that made me love you? You know quite well I have loved you for years and years! And then you talk of going away in silence and leaving me free and happy. Carlino, I'm ashamed of you!'

Like two children, they forgot for a little while the dark future, and basked in the sunny present. Parting was a thought hardly to be conceived while they sat together in the old Temple of Venus, and made love to each other after the fashion of lovers in all ages and climes.

After a time they talked of Carlo's future life, he spoke warmly of Sardoni, quoted Piale's high opinion of Marioni, the conductor, and said all that could be said in Merlino's favour. He wanted to paint his new life in bright colours for her sake, and he talked cheerfully of winning Nita's love and confidence, speaking with more assurance than he really felt.

And yet Francesca remembered well enough his words a few weeks before about the wretched, roving life of a singer, and she knew that in his heart he shrank from it still.

'Shall you be in Italy, do you think?' she asked.

'No,' replied Carlo, with a sigh. 'Merlino

will only stay here till he has got his chorus together again, and given his principals a short holiday. You see things are different here, travelling companies are not much in vogue.'

'Then, where will you be?'

'In England for a time, then in America.'

'America!' she could not repress the exclamation. 'That will seem terribly far away— I hoped, as they had just come back, there would be no question of going there again.'

'America is the great field for companies like Merlino's; I suppose a great deal of my life will probably be spent there.'

Francesca sighed.

'Ah, well, after all it is chiefly in imagination that distance affects one—our letters will travel just as well across the Atlantic. You will have to send me all your changes of address, Carlino; and, as for me, I shall have to learn to write smaller, or there will never be space enough for all I shall have to say.'

By the time the rest of the party joined them, they had grown accustomed to the thought of the change — had bravely faced the coming separation, each strengthening the other to endure; and Mr. Britton little guessed, as he gaily teased his niece about her indifference to the new discoveries, what had passed during that hour in the Temple of Venus. Francesca only smiled and drew him into a description of all they had seen, while with her eyes she followed rather wistfully the lithe figure running with Sibyl down the steep old street which led out of Pompeii. They lunched in the little restaurant at the entrance; allowed Mr. Britton to be inveigled into the region of photographs, bronzes, and lava ornaments; then, in the cool of the afternoon, drove home again, Francesca nursing a *Dying Gladiator* in terra-cotta, which was to go home to Clare in the *Pilgrim*.

If Captain Britton thought Carlo rather more silent than usual he put it down to constraint in the presence of a stranger,—the last thing Carlo would have been likely to experience. However, the worthy Captain liked him all the better for it, and talked to him in his bland, semi-patronising way, chaffing him not a little on his light-hearted compatriots who thronged the road in their *festa* clothes, closely packed in open carriages.

'Yes, yes; you Neapolitans are terrible pleasure-lovers,' he said, laughingly. 'Look there, now—ten people stowed away in that, and the horses all decked out with brass ornaments and bells; and yet they are people of the lower class who, likely enough, will be hungry to-morrow!'

Francesca fully expected that the term, 'lower class,' would call forth a remonstrance from Carlo, but he let it pass, and the next moment she understood why. His eye had been caught by a poster on one of the walls of Portici in which Madame Merlino's name appeared in large letters.

Carlo was invited to dine at the Casa Bella that evening; he had not yet made up his mind whether he would tell all to Captain Britton face to face, or whether he would write him a letter. Though a very fluent speaker, he was not particularly fond of writing English, however; and if only a favourable opportunity could be found he rather inclined to an interview with the Captain.

The opportunity came. Dessert was over,

Francesca had left the room, Mr. Britton excused himself soon after, as he had a great number of letters to write; the Captain drew his chair up to the table again and passed the wine to his guest. Carlo knew then that his time was come; the hand with which he helped himself to snow trembled a little, but his voice was firm and well modulated when he spoke.

'It seems a little ungracious to be glad that Mr. Britton's holiday should be invaded by business letters,' he began, 'but I particularly wanted a few words alone with you.'

Captain Britton thought of his scheme for hastening on the marriage, and quite hoped that the same idea had occurred to Carlo. A kindly smile played about his broad mouth.

'I, too, have wanted to speak with you all day, but these family parties are no time for confidential talk.'

Carlo thought of the Temple of Venus, and was silent. Captain Britton resumed:—

'The fact is I am anxious about you, my dear fellow; you look to me far from well. I wish that sister of yours was at the other side of the

Atlantic, and that's the truth of it; it was a bad day for all of us when she returned. When do they leave Naples? You'll never be yourself again till you are rid of that brother-in-law.'

'I am not likely to be rid of him for some time to come, I fear,' said Carlo, plunging boldly into his subject. 'It is about the step which I purpose taking that I wish now to speak to you.'

Did he mean to propose that wedding journey which the Captain had planned? His face was grave almost to sternness, but then the Merlinos were quite enough to account for that.

'I know it is a step which you will disapprove,' resumed Carlo. 'And yet—there is no help for it—take it I must.'

Captain Britton's hopes sank; he began to think apprehensively of all the things he should least like to happen.

'Well, short of turning Romanist again,' he said, after a pause, 'I don't think anything you are likely to do would disquiet me very much.'

'It will, however, delay our marriage,' said Carlo; 'that is, I fear, quite inevitable.'

'Well, well,' said Captain Britton, thinking

that he meant to study for some of the higher branches of the law, 'you are both young, and I can assure you I'm in no hurry to get rid of my little Francesca. Have you discussed the matter with her?'

'Yes, and she agrees with me that I must go.'

'Go! Where?'

'With Merlino's company; it is the only way in which I can keep my promise to my mother—the only possible way of shielding Anita.'

Captain Britton was so much startled that for a minute he could not speak, only the colour rose to his forehead and his eyes opened wider. In all his trouble and anxiety Carlo could not help observing that he bore a comical resemblance to the crimson shade over the lamp, with its owl's head and round, staring eyes. How was he to make this man, of all men in the world, understand Nita's position and sympathise with its difficulties? While he hesitated how best to put her case without divulging too much, the Captain recovered his breath.

'Do I understand that you mean to turn actor?' he asked in a sort of hoarse roar.

Tone and manner were alike overbearing.

Carlo made one of his dignified little bows and said gravely, 'Merlino has offered me reasonable terms, and Piale has long wished that I should go on the stage. Had I only my own wishes to consult I should certainly not choose the career of a public singer; but, sir, I promised my mother to shield Anita, and I must do my best—I must think of her.'

'I should have thought you were bound to think of your promised wife,' said the Captain, wrathfully, 'to consult her wishes.'

'Francesca agrees with me,' said Carlo; 'she would never keep me back from a duty.'

'Francesca is a fool, then. Duty, indeed! A duty to mix yourself up with a set of idle, profligate fellows! A duty to pander to the taste of the dissolute, and play the buffoon on the stage, and be clapped by all the scum of the town!'

Carlo by a great effort strangled the words of angry remonstrance which rose to his lips, and tried to understand the feelings of an Englishman with Puritan traditions. He would at least try to explain the state of affairs patiently.

'It is very hard for me to understand the view you take of the stage, sir,' he began; 'we Italians honour and respect our theatre; it is not, as you would say, the haunt of the dissolute, but the resort of the whole people——'

The Captain interrupted him, he was all the more angry because his companion had managed, so far, to exercise a well-bred restraint. Some devil prompted him to rouse the Italian's latent passion.

'Yes,' he said sneeringly, 'I know your national tendencies well enough, but I had thought you were superior to your countrymen. I see I was wrong; you are as frivolous and pleasure-seeking as the rest of the lot; it was well said of you Italians that you were only fit for artists' models and the operatic stage.'

Carlo sprang to his feet, fire flashing from his eyes.

'No man is called on to sit still and hear his country insulted,' he cried. 'The words are not worthy of you, sir; I am sure you will retract them.'

'If I retract them in part I certainly still

apply them to you,' said Captain Britton. 'What have you proved yourself but fickle and frivolous? You have altogether deceived me.'

His patriotic feelings somewhat smoothed, Carlo grew a little calmer, the personalities were less intolerable. Again he made an effort patiently to put before the Captain the whole case; this time he was determined that he would make him fully comprehend it and hear it out.

'You condemn me, sir, before you have grasped the situation,' he began, his voice so subdued by the strong restraint he was putting on himself that it sounded low and monotonous. In words plain enough to make the Englishman wince he briefly described the dilemma. 'Knowing this,' he went on,—'knowing, too, that my mother trusted to me to avert the danger, you surely cannot judge me harshly for taking this step. I knew the stage was dishonourable in your eyes, but I thought you would see in time that for me it was a necessity.'

The Captain had risen, too, and was pacing the room with quick, irritated steps. Nita's story had been a severe shock to him, Carlo's plain-speaking still caused his ears to tingle, and the thought of any sort of connection with a family on the borders of such a scandal was unbearable to him. He had a just pride in his Britton ancestry, in his honest, God-fearing forefathers; his strong love of family, his sense of kinship, was the best part of the man. But virtues generally have their corresponding vices, and the Captain had an overweening idea of his own dignity, and a habit of looking on other men's affairs from a lofty height, which often made his judgment faulty.

He was blind now to Carlo's unselfishness, blind to his pain, he struck out remorselessly, thinking only how to rescue Francesca from further connection with Madame Merlino's brother.

'Don't talk to me of duty and necessity,' he thundered; 'you are a Jesuit in disguise, you are doing evil that good may come, if, indeed, there is any thought of good in the whole plan. My own belief is that you are tired of Francesca. If so you couldn't have set to work better. I shall certainly not give my daughter in marriage to an actor; you may consider your betrothal at an end.'

For a minute the blow seemed to crush the very life out of Carlo, he turned deathly white. Twice he made as though he would speak, twice failed in the attempt, his lips refusing to frame the words. Captain Britton felt a pang of regret as he saw the result of his own work, but the regret was soon swallowed up in wrathful recollections.

'I don't think you in your heart believe all that you say of me, sir,' said Donati, struggling even now to make excuse for Francesca's father. 'All I can do is to bow to your decision. You will let me see Francesca?'

Something in his patient dignity, in his manly forbearance, struck a hard blow at the Captain's pride. What a contrast there was between his own behaviour and the behaviour of the Italian! The thought chafed him, and called forth a burst of passionate anger.

'I shall not dream of permitting you to see her,' he cried furiously. 'I'll have no more of your kissing and caressing for my daughter, you'll have enough of that at the theatre. Keep your caresses for the *prima donnas!* '

In an instant Carlo's whole bearing altered, the burning colour rushed to his cheeks, his eyes blazed, all his pent-up wrath burst forth like a volcano. For an Italian nature is not unlike the Mediterranean itself; people are tempted to presume on that calm, blue peacefulness which looks as if it could never be broken, and then they find themselves suddenly overtaken by one of its sharp, characteristic storms; and, just in the same way, they presume on the infinite patience and the sweet nature of those Southerners whose only wish it has seemed to please, and are amazed when they find that sensitiveness and delicacy of perception has two sides.

Captain Britton had at length exhausted even the patience and courtesy of an Italian; he was alarmed now at the storm he had evoked.

Carlo's English had forsaken him, his voice, so subdued a minute before, was now eager and passionate, his gesticulations were vehement as he poured forth a torrent of angry remonstrance, a storm of words so rapidly uttered that to foreign ears they were hardly intelligible.

The Captain was only conscious of two things: that he deserved this burst of indignation, and that he must somehow get rid of his fiery guest. At such a moment, and in such agitation, he was not likely to weigh his words. At length Carlo paused for a moment, not because his wrath had cooled, but because his breath failed him. The Captain instantly snatched at his advantage.

'I will at least save my child from further contact with a deceiver!' he exclaimed hoarsely. 'She is mine, and I owe it to her to shield her from such as you.' They were words which could never be forgotten,—words which in their cruel injustice would rankle like a poisoned arrow. The same white-heat of passion which causes daily murders in the Santa Lucia district leapt now to Carlo's brain, yet through it all he was conscious of a voice in his heart which said, 'Go, go at once while you can control your limbs. Go while there is yet time.'

The habit of a lifetime prevailed; to turn

and leave his foe was to him more bitter than death, but with a struggle worthy of his brave progenitors, he obeyed the voice, and strode out of the room without a word.

He did not dare to pause for a moment, lest he should see Francesca, or perhaps hear her voice in the distance and be overcome. With hurried steps he crossed the vestibule, snatched up his hat from the stand, flung his coat across his chest, and closed the door of Casa Bella behind him. Then he stopped for a minute, suddenly conscious that he felt sick and giddy, and that he was still trembling with passion. The fiend whom he had worsted assailed him in a new form.

'You treated him with great forbearance,' it argued; 'you proved yourself his superior in every way. He ought to apologise to you for what he said.'

Carlo walked slowly home. The idea of bringing the Englishman to his feet and making him crave pardon soothed him a little. 'This anger shall not get the mastery of me,' he said to himself. 'I will go in and make my preparations for leaving home just as if this had not happened.'

And, with the sort of unreal strength which anger gives, he actually did begin his sorrowful task, called the servants together, told them that he was leaving Italy, paid them their wages, and dismissed them. Then, more tried by the sight of their grief and surprise than he had fancied would be the case, he sat down to his desk and began to write letters. There was the lease of the Villa Bruno to be disposed of, it was his for another year; he wrote to a house-agent in Naples. There was the furniture to be sold; he wrote to an auctioneer, asking that an early date might be fixed for the sale. At any other time these letters would have cost him much to write, but now he felt little, for fierce anger crowded out grief and regret. He had not in the least realised that he was never again to see Francesca; he could realise nothing but that he had been insulted,—grossly insulted, by the man who should have been his best friend. And yet, though he was still beside himself with passion, he was all the time aware of an inner voice urging him to forgive. The idea made him laugh scornfully as he directed and stamped his envelopes. What! was he to forgive one so clearly in the wrong? He had never before felt the difficulty of forgiving, being naturally generous and sweet-tempered; but Captain Britton had wounded him too deeply. Words which might have been pardoned in a mere acquaintance, seemed unpardonable in a friend who had known him from boyhood. The recollection of them sent another of those maddening bursts of fury through his frame. He pushed back his chair and began to pace the room, wrestling with the demon of fierce hatred which possessed him. For Francesca's sake he could have forgiven her father almost anything, but so gross an insult to his love—the love which he knew to be pure, and sacred, and unblamable—was surely beyond forgiveness.

It was only slowly and by degrees that he began to reap the fruits of his brave struggle for self-mastery. He grew a little calmer, and turned from the torturing recollection of the insult to an inward picture of Captain Britton himself. Almost dispassionately he began to consider that big, broad, massive figure, that bluff, weather-beaten face, with its calculating, far-seeing eyes and wide mouth. Genial and friendly as he had hitherto thought the Captain to be, he had never given him credit for much refinement of feeling; he had known well enough that the Englishman found it very hard to make allowance for anything outside his own circle; he had long been fain to admit in his own heart what he would never have admitted, even to Enrico Ritter, that there was in Francesca's father a slight but unmistakable vein of vulgarity. It was, then, only too natural that the Captain should fail to understand the present state of things, and, so failing, should supply hideous motives for so unaccountable a step. Oh, yes, it was natural enough. He ought to have been prepared for it. But the perception of this brought him no nearer to forgiveness.

The night was now far advanced, but sleep was out of the question in his present state. He began to roam through the house, considering what things he should save from the sale; some were too precious to be lost, and must be left to Enrico's keeping; some were small enough to be reserved as souvenirs of home, to be taken away on his wanderings. Going up to his bedroom, his eye fell at once upon his father's sword, which hung above the mantelpiece, and beneath it a childish device of his own—a golden shield, and upon it, in red letters, the name of each battle in which the sword had been used. 'Aspromonte,' in larger letters curving up to the left and right to meet the shape of the shield, shone out conspicuously.

'I'll not be parted from that,' he said to himself, a thrill of loving reverence passing through him and killing the anger and hatred. 'I shall, perhaps, need a sword in my stage wardrobe, and so, after all, this will be needed to protect Nita. It would seem like desecration to the Captain to use it on the stage, yet it will surely be my own fault if it is less honourable than at Aspromonte.'

His thoughts wandered back to that last vividly remembered scene beside his father's death-bed, and a glow of eager devotion warmed his heart as he pledged himself anew to keep that promise, to go forth bravely as the knights of old in defence of the weak and the tempted, to live the life of the Crucified.

Then, like lightning, it suddenly flashed upon him how grievously he had failed. Self had started to the front even in his self-sacrifice; he had borne but a few strokes from the enemy, and at the first personal insult had thrown down his colours; reviled, he had reviled again; suffering, he had threatened; wounded, he had sought to wound. In anguish he remembered that flood of scathing words, that fiery retort which had escaped him; and yet there was One who had borne the worst possible insults in strong silence, and he had vowed that he would live His life! Instead, he had suffered himself to be overcome by an unjust judgment, to be maddened by a few words spoken by a man who had also yielded to the same devil of pride and anger. How was he to face the difficulties of life in Merlino's troupe when at the very outset his temper had betrayed him? In bitter grief and self-reproach he had to learn, as all of us have to learn, that 'We must be humbled utterly in our own conceits before we can be peacemakers.'

After a while, he was seized with that strong desire to start afresh which comes to every wounded soldier, whether he fights in the legions of the Seen or the Unseen. His share of the wrong must first be set right; that was as clear as it was hard. He doubted if he could bring himself to do it, but he went so far as to go down to the *salotto*, take out his desk, and sit down with pen and paper before him. And at length, just as faint golden streaks appeared in the horizon heralding the day, the letter was finished and the struggle over.

Carlo could not rest till he had done all that could be done, so he went out into the cold dawn, and, making his way to the Casa Bella, dropped his missive in the letter-box. Then, when all was over, when he knew that for the last time he was leaving the house which contained all that he loved, his desolation suddenly broke upon him. Wrath had stilled grief, but now that his anger had passed Grief claimed him for her own. His betrothal was at an end; Francesca was no longer his; even a farewell was denied him. With heart-broken wonder he marvelled how it was that only now did he fully take-in the idea. What was Captain Britton? What were all the insults in the world before the one bitter, desolating fact that he was parted from his love?

How he got home he never knew, but he vaguely remembered finding his way to his own room, and seeing through a mist the sword and the red letters of 'Aspromonte' beneath. Then, in his great anguish, he had cried aloud, 'Strengthen me, O God! that I, too, may be faithful till death.'

But, afterwards, all was a blank, and when he came to himself the sun was far above the horizon, and he was lying at full length on the floor, feeling stiff, and sore, and bruised.

CHAPTER XII.

A TROUBLED NIGHT.

> 'Ah, Love! but a day,
>   And the world is changed!
> The sun's away,
>   And the bird estranged;
> The wind has dropped,
>   And the sky's deranged;
> Summer has stopped.
>
> R. BROWNING.

FRANCESCA kept up bravely all through the long hours of that Whitsun Monday; at dinner she talked a little more than usual to cover Carlo's silence, but it was hard work, and she gave a sigh of relief when at length the ordeal was over, and she was free to go away alone. Carlo stood up to open the door for her, and as she passed him she looked up into his eyes and smiled; but once within the friendly shelter of the drawing-room her own filled with tears. She would have given much to run up to her room and have a good cry; that was out of the question, however, for she could not plead a headache when by doing so she should lose Carlo's good night. The sound of the dining-room door opening made her beat a hasty retreat from the lamplight; she stood in the shade, and made as though she were looking out of the window, while she hurriedly dried her eyes, for not for the world would she have been caught crying. Mr. Britton, coming into the room, descried the slim figure in its black lace dress, and came towards her.

'My sweet Fran,' he said, 'if you will not think me the laziest old uncle in the world, I am going to bid you good-night. Here is a budget of letters which I shall get through better in my own room.'

'Must you really see to them now?' she said. 'Why, it is not half a holiday if business follows you out here.'

Something in her voice made him look at her more attentively. He saw that she was in trouble, recollected that Carlo had scarcely spoken to her through dinner, and very naturally leapt to the conclusion that there had been a quarrel between the lovers.

'I have a long letter from Kate, which perhaps you'll like to see,' he said. 'She and Clare seem getting on grandly at the North Cape. They know nothing of your betrothal. May I tell them the news when I answer this?'

'I think I will tell them myself,' she said, her colour deepening a little. 'I will put in a line to-morrow, if I may.'

The tears welled up into her eyes again; she turned hastily and drew his attention to the distant view of Vesuvius with crimson flame leaping up, and summer lightning brightening the sky in the background. But Mr. Britton was too fond of her to be put aside; he began to feel really anxious about her future.

'Dear little niece,' he said, gently, 'you must forgive an old uncle's anxiety, but are you quite happy in your betrothal? Are you quite sure that you have chosen the happiest life?'

'I am sure that I have chosen the only man in the world whom I could love,' she said, recovering herself, and looking up into her uncle's face with such a sweet, bright, lovelit smile that he could only inwardly protest that no man living was worthy of her.

'Yet something is troubling you to-night?' he said, uneasily.

'Yes,' she said, her lips quivering; 'there is something troubling Carlo; he is going to talk it over with father, and—and I am not quite sure how father will take it.'

Mr. Britton looked grave.

'Dear child, of one thing you may at least be sure,' he said, gently; 'your father cares for nothing but your happiness.'

The words fitted in only too well with her own forebodings.

'Oh, why will people think of nothing but that?' she exclaimed. 'What is happiness to me when Carlo is in the question? Uncle'—she looked up at him appealingly—'promise me that whatever happens you will never think him to blame;—there are things no outsider can understand. Promise me that you will always be his friend.'

'Well, he must be a cold-hearted person who could refuse such a petition from such lips,' he said, stooping to kiss her. 'Don't be unhappy, dear little Fran; there never yet was a betrothal which was all sunshine. Wait a little, and your clouds will disperse. Nine o'clock! I must be off to my desk.'

'I will send up your coffee, then. Goodnight,' said Francesca, feeling a little comforted at having enlisted such a helper as Uncle George on Carlo's side.

She sat down near the lamp, and unfolded her cousin's letter, trying hard to feel some interest in the account of the voyage, and the midnight sun, and the adventures which always seemed to occur to anyone who travelled with Clare. But it would not do; the words conveyed nothing to her mind; she could only listen for the sound of approaching steps, for the long delay made her feel certain that Carlo was at that moment telling her father of his decision.

At length, after what seemed to her a very long time, she heard the dining-room door sharply opened and closed, then quick steps crossing the vestibule. She listened breathlessly, and, by a sudden impulse, started to her feet, but the next instant she sank down again almost as though someone had struck her, for she had heard the front door closed, and knew that her father must have forbidden Carlo to see her again.

After that she felt no inclination to cry, only a sense of cold and wretchedness,—a dull, aching misery. She sat crouched up on the sofa, still holding Kate's letter in her hand. Presently the clock struck ten, and the study bell was sharply rung. In a minute Dino appeared at the drawing-room door.

'Captain Britton is very busy, signorina,' said the old butler, 'and does not wish to be disturbed again to-night. He would be much obliged if the signorina would read prayers.'

The good old servant had no idea how much he conveyed to his young mistress in that commonplace message. The words cut her to the heart, but with the true womanly instinct to hide her wounds, she stood up quickly and said in her usual voice, 'Very well, Dino; bring in the books then.'

And steadily she went through the usual

form, her voice never once faltering, nor did she give way till the door of her own room was safely locked, and she was alone for that night of doubt, and suspense, and grief.

Meanwhile Captain Britton was not much happier than the two lovers whose separation he had decreed. He felt as soon as he had dismissed Dino that he had done a cowardly thing; but the thought of meeting Francesca that night, or of reading prayers in his present frame of mind, was more than he could endure.

At heart the Captain was a kind man; he would have liked to please all with whom he came in contact, if only they would be pleased in his own way; but to have his plans crossed, to be disappointed in any matter upon which he had set his heart, was too much for so proud a temper to bear.

Nor could he at all understand Carlo's knight-errantry. That a brother under the circumstances should be beside himself with anger, should afterwards give the traitor a good horse-whipping, or even challenge him—this he could have understood and approved; but the quiet surrender of home, country, profession, and personal happiness, in the hope of preventing the evil, this was altogether beyond him.

The Captain liked well enough to do a good action, but it must be an action that would be approved of men; nothing would have induced him to take a line that would expose him to censure: if he did a generous thing he would take good care that it should win him the pleasant and cheering approval of his friends and acquaintance.

And yet, in spite of his anger with Carlo's quixotic scheme, he was too kind-hearted a man not to regret the harsh and wholly unjustifiable words which had escaped him in the heat of the moment. Keen shame made the colour mount to his forehead as he remembered that he had insulted a guest at his own table. The thought of this troubled him more than anything. It haunted him all through the night. He regretted deeply the pain he must give to Francesca; he felt bitterly disappointed that the marriage should now be out of the question; he was still indignant with Carlo's blind foolishness in going on the stage: but everything faded into insignificance before the one great regret,— a regret which would follow the Captain to his grave,—that for once in his life he had been guilty of a breach of hospitality.

If sleep refused to visit either Carlo or Francesca that night, it was equally cruel to Captain Britton. He tossed and turned till the bedclothes were in a state of chaotic confusion: he tried the window open, he tried the window shut, he tried a light, he tried total darkness, he paced the room, he counted alternate black and white sheep going through a gate, he ate bread, he smoked a cigar,—in fact, he tried all the remedies for sleeplessness he had ever heard of.

At last he gave up all thoughts of rest for that night, and began to wonder how his neighbour was faring: the young Italian's face haunted him. Now he saw him boyish, eager, and impulsive, coming nearly five years ago to tell of his love for Francesca, and receiving his sentence of probation with an odd mixture of hope, despair, and courtesy. Again he recalled the day—only three weeks ago in reality, though it seemed more like three months—when Sibyl had run down to find him in the olive-garden, bearing that significant card with the words, 'Avvocato Carlo Poerio Donati,' which conveyed to him so much. He remembered hastening back to the house, and could see again in imagination the bright look of hope which had flashed like sudden sunshine over Carlo's face when he had told him to go and find Francesca in the belvedere. And then, lastly, and most vividly of all, he recalled that face as he had last seen it. Such anger once seen is never forgotten; and the Captain knew that so generous and sweet-tempered a man must have been almost maddened by pain before his face could have worn that look of vindictive fury, before his eyes could have blazed with the fierce glow that recalled to him the eyes of a wounded lion. Had the Captain been a coward, or even a man with highly-strung nerves, he would have trembled before such a look, for to meet such eyes is to look death in the face. But, with all his faults, he was a staunch, brave-hearted Englishman, and all that he had felt was a great surprise when the fierce gleam had suddenly died away, and Carlo had turned sharply round on his heel and left him without a word.

He wondered what had happened to him afterwards, and began to feel troubled as he remembered the desolateness of the Villa Bruno.

Only a fortnight had passed since the gentle Signora Donati had been laid in her grave; he had forgotten all that when in sudden wrath he had driven her son away. Bitterly did he now repent the unkindness. Had he been an imaginative man, he would have conjured up a tragic ending to that night's work, and have suffered yet more; but, luckily, he was not of an imaginative turn, so he was only vaguely and increasingly miserable.

Then he began to think of poor little Francesca, doomed through his angry command never to see her lover again. No; at least he would yield on that point, he would go to see Carlo after breakfast, would apologise to him for his hastiness, and permit him to come once more to the Casa Bella and take leave of Francesca. This idea gave the poor Captain a little relief, but he groaned aloud as he thought of all the grief in store for his child.

At length he heard the welcome sounds of life in the house. The night was over; Rosetta was banging the door-mat vigorously against the porch; Dino was tramping up and down the marble passages, fetching and carrying. Presently there was the refreshing sound of the rap at his door, and the servant's familiar summons, 'Half-past seven, signor, and a fine morning.'

The Captain rose more promptly than usual, unlocked his door, and took in his hot-water can; on the lid there lay an envelope directed to him in Carlo's handwriting. He tore it open with a sense of sickening anxiety.

What was it that brought a sudden mist before his eyes? Only a short, manly letter,—a letter of apology from the man whom he had wronged.

Carlo had forestalled him, and the letter which had cost the writer so much cost the reader yet more. There was very little in it, with its careful English and neat foreign writing; but the words had come straight from the heart, and they went straight as an arrow to the heart of the Captain.

The Brittons, though so long resident in Italy, kept English hours and breakfasted all together at eight o'clock.

The Captain came down that morning with a curiously guilty feeling. Francesca was in the dining-room before him, apparently absorbed in coffee-making. He glanced at her anxiously, and saw that she was pale and worn, and looked as if she had cried till she could cry no longer. She felt her father's anxious glance and winced beneath it. Uncle George, with more tact, made as though he noticed nothing, and adroitly kept the conversation going; while Sibyl was luckily at that unobservant age which takes no account of faces when once they have become familiar. It was an uncomfortable meal, and they all hailed as a relief the appearance of the Captain of the *Pilgrim*, a weather-beaten Scotchman, who had driven over with a telegram which had just arrived for Mr. Britton.

Captain Britton had never felt more glad to have a guest to whom he could show hospitality.

'Come, Captain, you must breakfast with us after your long drive!' he exclaimed, in his hearty voice. 'Sibyl, run and tell Dino to lay another place.'

'Thank you, sir,' said the Captain, drawing a chair to the table; 'I breakfasted on the yacht, but I will be glad of a cup of coffee if Miss Britton has some for a late comer. I thought I'd better come over with the telegram, sir,' he continued, turning to the owner of the *Pilgrim*, 'for I had a feeling it might mean a change of plans.'

'Second-sight on your part, Captain,' said Mr. Britton, looking up; 'I am sorry to say it does mean a change of plans and an end to my holiday. I must go home at once.'

'Nothing wrong at Merlebank, I hope?' said his brother, while Francesca and Sibyl listened anxiously.

'Oh, no; it is only a business affair, but I must be home by Friday at latest. I'm afraid the *Pilgrim* would hardly manage that, Captain, eh?'

There was a general laugh.

'Well, that would be expecting a little too much of a sailing yacht,' said Captain Graham.

'I'm sorry, sir, you are called back to England. We had looked to have a pleasant cruise.'

Mr. Britton sighed.

'No peace to the wicked; eh, Francesca? In this world it is always the way that some people have more work than they wish, and others not so much. I should like a few words with you, John, in the study.'

The brothers went off together, and the old Scotch Captain turned to Sibyl.

'What should you say to a cruise, Miss Sibyl? I think that would be just the thing for you. You'd make a fine little sailor.'

'Oh, dear Captain Graham, do coax Uncle George to let me!' cried Sibyl, in an ecstasy. 'Oh, Fran, wouldn't it be lovely!'

Francesca smiled faintly, not wishing to damp the little girl's pleasure, but feeling a little more wretched than before, as she wondered whether possibly her father might think it best to send her away from home.

'Sea air would do you all the good in the world, miss,' said Captain Graham, glancing at her pale face; 'it's only a pity none of your cousins are on board, then we should have a merry party. Miss Kate, she doesn't care for the yacht, but the others, why, they are as good as sailors! Miss Lucy and Miss Molly, they kept a watch all through our last cruise; and as to little Miss Flo, why, she'd like to live on board.'

Meanwhile, in the study, the owner of the *Pilgrim* was trying to do all in his power for his pretty niece. He had guessed, both from her face and his brother's depression, that there must have been a quarrel with young Donati on the previous night. He hoped he might be able to set things straight again before he left, but he had no idea how serious was the state of affairs.

'Look here, John,' he said, closing the door of the study, 'it has just struck me, why shouldn't you all have a trip in the yacht now she is here? There will be plenty of room for you, and the girls, and young Donati, and a couple of other friends besides, if you like. Now do think of it, for it quite vexes me that the *Pilgrim* should be all down here to no purpose.'

'You are very good,' said Captain Britton, hesitatingly; 'for myself there is nothing I should so much like; indeed, I must get away somewhere, I feel quite knocked up with this tiresome affair.'

'What affair?'

'Why, I meant to have told you all about it to-day. Poor little Francesca's engagement is broken off!'

'Dear me! how is that? You don't mean to say he is tired of her already?'

'No, that's the worst of it; the fellow is desperately in love with her still, but I have had to put a stop to it. I never was so disappointed in a man in my life.'

'It's a grave affair,' said Mr. Britton, thoughtfully, 'for I fancy little Fran's heart is quite given away.'

'That is the miserable part of it. I wish she had never seen Donati! I wish I'd never come to this place!' and the poor Captain sighed heavily.

'But have you not, perhaps, been a trifle hasty?' said his brother, remembering the promise he had made to Francesca on the previous night. 'Though starting with plenty of insular prejudice against the man I was very much struck with him yesterday. There is something noble about his face. Surely he can't be guilty of any great offence?'

'He is guilty of the greatest offence possible, he is guilty of an utter want of common-sense,' said the Captain, angrily. 'I thought we had made half an Englishman of him, but I might have known that with his Italian blood and his foolish radical ideas we should, sooner or later, fall foul of one another.'

'You are surely not going to break off the engagement because of political differences?' said Mr. Britton, getting quite on to the wrong tack.

'Mere opinions are nothing to me,' said the Captain, 'but when the fellow acts—acts upon his insane ideas—comes to me and deliberately tells me that he has taken a course which will make his marriage with Francesca out of the question for an indefinite time, what can you expect me to say?'

'I don't wonder you were very much vexed about it.'

'Vexed! I was never in such a heat in my life. Wrong as the fellow was, I am bound to apologise to him for what I said. I'll not shirk that, though I do believe the mere sight of him will put me out of temper again.'

'You think there is no hope, then, of setting matters straight? Surely you would submit to almost anything rather than put Francesca to so much pain. What if her lover is a little high-flown in his notions? Anything is better than callousness and indifference.'

'I can't explain it all to you, for did I do so I should break Donati's confidence, but soon you will see for yourself what line he has taken up, and then you will see that my anger is at least excusable. To permit the engagement to go on is out of the question while he still keeps to his resolution; Miss Claremont, I am sure, would agree with me. He is deliberately choosing a career which is bound to degrade him—he is taking the high road to hell.'

The Captain was working himself up into

wrathful indignation again. Mr. Britton could only imagine that Donati had avowed his connection with some secret political society such as he believed to exist in Italy. He saw that it was useless to attempt any further remonstrance.

'Then, if this is really quite at an end,' he said, hesitatingly, 'would it not be doubly desirable that you should all leave the neighbourhood for a time? Take a month's cruise in the *Pilgrim*. There is no chance of my using her again till August.'

'I wish you could have been with us too,' said the Captain, with a sigh. 'Must you really go off at once?'

'I must be off this evening, there's no help for it,' said Mr. Britton. 'I would give much to be with you, but this business will bear no delay—I feel like a school-boy cheated of his holiday. But look, let us decide this matter while Captain Graham is here. When would you like to start?'

'To-morrow;—no. To-morrow Count Carossa dines with us,—but on Thursday,—I really think we might start on Thursday. It's very good of you, George, to propose it. You've no idea what a relief it will be to me, for we are such near neighbours to Donati that it would be very unpleasant to be here.'

'Well, that's settled, then,' said Mr. Britton. 'I'll go and tell Graham to make preparation for you. He will be enchanted to have you on board.'

CHAPTER XIII.

'PAZIENZA.'

'We may not make this world a paradise
By walking it together, hand in hand,
With eyes that meeting feed a double strength.
We must be only joined by pains divine
Of spirits blent in mutual memories.'
Spanish Gipsy.

CAPTAIN BRITTON had seldom felt more ill at ease than when he walked that morning up to the door of the Villa Bruno. A sallow, wrinkled, old servant, with a gay scarlet neckerchief, was polishing the door-handle; she nodded to him cheerfully as he approached.

'Good-morning to you, signor; walk in. You'll find the master in the *salotto.*'

She made no sign of leaving her door-handle and duster, and indeed the Captain had long ago asked leave to walk into his neighbour's house without ceremony, and the Signora Donati and Carlo, though disliking his unheralded intrusion, had been far too courteous to return a negative to the tactless request. He crossed the vestibule and was about to enter the *salotto* when a sound of voices within made him pause, hesitate a moment, and then go instead into an adjoining room.

He had recognised the voice of Guido Donati, and guessed correctly that the uncle had driven over in hot haste from Naples on learning his nephew's startling plan. That he was exceedingly annoyed could be gathered from the tone of his voice and from the vehement and extraordinarily rapid utterance, which reminded the Captain of Carlo's tirade on the preceding night. At last the violent harangue came to an end, and Carlo's voice was heard: it was low but distinct, and the Captain could not avoid hearing the words,—

'I am sorry to vex you, uncle, but my mind is made up.'

'*Madonna Santissima!* it is made up, is it?' said the other, furiously. 'Then mine, too, is made up; and I am sorry to vex you, but not a penny of mine shall you ever inherit. Do you understand?'

There was a silence, but Captain Britton could well imagine the expressive gesture which Carlo would make.

'*Diavolo!*' cried the uncle. 'You take it calmly. You think you will live comfortably enough on that voice of yours, and laugh at the rich old uncle. You will tell a different tale a few years hence, my fine fellow, when you have a wife and children to support!'

'I shall never marry,' said Carlo, speaking more shortly than the Captain had ever before heard an Italian speak.

'What?' cried Uncle Guido. 'Then you have thrown over your betrothal for this mad scheme? An apoplexy on you! I'll have no more to do with such a fool;' and with that he strode out of the room.

The Captain only waited till he was sure the angry man had really gone, and then he knocked at the door of the *salotto*. Nothing but a conscientious sense of duty could have induced him to face at that moment his guest of the previous evening; but there was a certain rugged loyalty about Francesca's father, and he walked sturdily into the room, bracing himself up to make the necessary apology. Carlo was standing at the side window, the sunlight fell full upon him, and revealed to the Captain a very different face to the one which had haunted him through the night — a face worn with suffering, but strong and resolute, spite of its haggard look.

'I beg your pardon for intruding, but the servant told me to come in,' began the Captain, approaching him.

Carlo turned with an inarticulate exclamation, the blood rushed to his face, and a look of distress dawned in his eyes; he was tired out with all he had been through, and felt wholly unequal to another stormy discussion.

But he welcomed his visitor with native ceremoniousness, betraying only by additional courtesy any remembrance of the quarrel. The Captain remembered the letter of the morning, and all his kindly feelings returned to him, as he said heartily,—

'Carlo, I have come to apologise for the words which escaped me yesterday. I regret them more than I can tell you. You had every excuse for your anger.'

Carlo grasped his hand. 'No, no,' he said, quickly, 'I was very much to blame. I am glad, sir—it is a great relief to me—that last night was not our parting. I am grateful to you for coming here to-day.'

'I must also apologise for having inadvertently overheard some of your uncle's words,' said the Captain, who felt very uncomfortable when he remembered his involuntary eavesdropping.

'I knew Uncle Guido would be very much against this plan,' said Carlo; and as he spoke he threw himself wearily into a chair facing Captain Britton's.

The Captain was struck by the look of extreme physical exhaustion both in the face and the attitude; he began to realise the difference between his own physique and that of the Italian, and faintly to understand that Carlo had a greater capacity for feeling pain than he had himself.

'Did you realise that this scheme of yours—this scheme which I still most strongly dis-

approve—would cost you so dear?' he asked
abruptly. 'Did you think your uncle would
have disinherited you?'

'I didn't think about the money at all,'
said Carlo; 'but I knew he would be annoyed.'

'But does this make no change in your
feeling? Are you willing to lose every single
thing you possess, and even to forfeit the
respect of your friends, for the sake of this
plan?'

'Yes,' he said simply; 'I am willing, sir.'

When he had spoken he let his head drop
wearily on to his hand; he was calm with the
calm of blank bereavement, for, like the Princess
in the poem, he had found that

> 'Not to fear because all is taken
> Is the loneliest depth of human pain.'

The Captain sighed. He was not angry
now, only very much annoyed at the impossibility of inducing one bereft of common-sense
to see reason.

'You make light of the loss of income,'
he said at length; 'but how will you fare
supposing you fall ill?'

Carlo looked up with an odd sort of smile.

'Well, you will think me unpractical,' he said; 'but I have never been ill in my life, and I had not considered that possibility. However my salary is a tolerably fair one for a novice, and if the worst comes to the worst there are always the hospitals.'

'Carlo,' broke in the Captain, 'I can't bear to think of one who has led the life you have led going out into such a world! What would your poor mother have said to it?'

Carlo's face lighted up as if the suggestion had given him some unexpected comfort.

'At least our dead understand us,' he said, fervently; 'they know that I am trying to keep my promise.'

The Captain felt that his small stock of patience would not last much longer, and Carlo, glancing at him, saw that their parting, though peaceable, would be final; he knew intuitively that although the Captain had taken back some of his harsh words, he still regarded him as at any rate a self-deceived deceiver, a man who under the cloak of duty veiled his craving for change and excitement, or, at best, as an enthusiast who could but be despised for giving up solid realities for foolish dreams. Their friendship was at an end; for, though love is undying, friendship is quite a different thing, and there are shocks which it will not survive.

'There is one other thing I wished to say,' said Captain Britton, rising, 'and that is, that if you wish you may have one more interview with Francesca.'

Carlo caught eagerly at this boon, and the Captain suggested that he should return with him to Casa Bella.

'Does she know of——' he hesitated how to put it, 'of your decision?'

'I have not spoken to her about it, but I know she infers it,' said the Captain, rather coldly.

Carlo paced the room for a minute, struggling with his emotion; he was not sure whether he had strength to meet Francesca and tell her with his own lips that all was over between them.

'If you wish to see her we had better come

at once,' said the Captain. 'My brother is unexpectedly called back to England, and we have much to see to to-day.'

He was vexed that Donati did not show more gratitude for the concession he had made, for he was a man who liked to be thanked, and it had not been easy for him to retract what he had first said. Something in his tone stung Carlo; he drew himself together. '*Ebbene, signor*,' he said gravely, forgetting his English, as he often did when much moved, and recovering it with an effort. 'If you will permit it I will accompany you.'

They walked away from the Villa Bruno in silence, Carlo thinking of the Captain's words, 'We have much to see to to-day.' How calmly he classed the supreme struggle of his life, the parting that was as death to him, with the trivial household commotion caused by Mr. Britton's journey.

But once back in his own house the Captain's kinder feelings returned; he took Carlo to the rose-room, then held out his hand cordially.

'This had better be our final parting,' he

said, 'I leave home on Thursday. Good-bye, Carlo. Should you even now see fit to give up this foolish scheme I should be quite willing to reconsider matters.'

'My mind is made up, sir,' said Carlo, turning sadly away.

'So it appears. Well, I will send Francesca to you.'

He closed the door; and Carlo, with a choking feeling in his throat, looked round the dear, familiar room, the very untidiness of which breathed of Francesca. The 'Dying Gladiator' for Clare reposed perilously on a shaky pile of books; a kitten was worrying a ball of red wool on the sofa; and the sock in process of knitting, and which he knew had been intended for him, lay at a little distance on the floor. He turned to the window, and looked out at his old friend Vesuvius with its cloud of smoke, and at the glimpses of blue sea visible here and there between the trees. Then, with an aching consciousness that these were left to him, but that he should never more stand in that little room, he turned and looked round it, as though he wished to stamp for ever on his mind all its girlish decorations, all its familiar details. But the sound of footsteps without roused him and dispelled his calm; the door opened, and Francesca came quickly forward to greet him; she always entered a room more quickly, yet more gracefully than other people, but now she almost ran towards him, she wanted him not to notice her wan, tear-stained face.

If, however, in one sense love is blind, in another it is all-observant; in one glance he had read all, and in that glance there came to him the sharpest of his suffering.

Stifling the sobs that rose in his throat he held her in a long, close embrace, but to speak was impossible; and though there was comfort and rapture in her presence, yet there was also anguish which threatened to unman him. At length he put her gently from him, and turned away that he might fight down his emotion. For a few minutes there was silence, then he came and sat beside her on the sofa, and, putting his arm round her, drew her head down on to his shoulder.

'*Carina,*' he said, and the mellow baritone voice was firm, yet terribly sad, 'your father would not let me see you last night, but to-day he allows me this one more meeting with you. He said he had not spoken to you, but that you knew what had passed between us.'

'Yes,' she said, her tears raining down quietly; 'I knew it must be so when I heard you go.'

They talked sometimes in English, sometimes in Italian, as had been their custom ever since childhood.

'Darling,' he said, tenderly, 'I am bound to obey your father's decree; there could be no right betrothal for us without his consent, and so you stand free once more. You must try, *carina,* not to let these three short weeks spoil your life; you will try, my own, my darling, for it would break my heart if I thought I had ruined your happiness.'

'Love ought not to weaken us,' she said tremulously, for in her heart she felt that apart from Carlo she should be like a rudderless boat. 'These three weeks ought to give me courage for the rest.'

There was indescribable sadness in the last two words.

'Ah, darling!' cried Carlo, passionately, 'don't speak of your beautiful young life like that!'

And then he was silent again. All the strength and ardour of their mutual love seemed to rise up against the Captain's decree; if for the present they were fain to obey it and to part, yet hopes for the future would rise; perhaps each intuitively knew what was in the other's heart, but no words passed between them; indeed when Carlo did speak it was almost as if he wished to reason away any brightness which might hover over their future.

'You see, my darling,' he said, 'even should this immediate danger no longer keep me from you, even if Nita no longer needed me, I shall have cut myself off from you hopelessly,—we must face that. I shall by that time, if I succeed at all, be to the world Donati the singer, and your father would certainly not choose me for his son-in-law. Then, again, Uncle Guido has disinherited me, so that if I gave up the stage I should be penniless and more or less unfitted for work as an advocate.'

'Has he indeed disinherited you? Oh, Carlino, what troubles you have had! Don't let me be another, darling. See, I'll not cry any more; we must think of what is still left us. The worst they can do to us is to keep us apart; they can't kill our love, they can't check our prayers for each other—the best part, the highest part no one can meddle with.'

He held her closely, murmuring tender Italian words of endearment; and the clock on the mantelpiece ticked on inexorably, measuring all too quickly the time which, when they were parted, would move with leaden feet. Rosalind should surely have said 'parting lovers' rather than a 'thief going to the gallows' when asked, 'Who gallops Time withal?' And still they lingered over the sweet, unwritable talk till the clock relentlessly struck twelve, and roused them to the recollection of the outer world.

Then Francesca drew off her engagement ring, and placed it in his hand.

'There, Carlo,' she said, steadily, 'I give you

back the ring and your troth, and I will obey my father, and will neither hear from you nor write to you; but more than that no woman can promise, for love is not made and unmade to order.'

Carlo put on the ring, which from a token of union had now become changed to a token of separation. He was too heart-broken to speak, and after a long pause it was Francesca who at length broke the silence.

'Tell me a little more of the sort of life you shall live,' she said, gently.

So he told her all that he knew, which was little enough; how he should live with the Merlinos, try to win his sister's love, study hard for his profession, do his best to be a credit to Piale.

'And you?' he asked. 'There will be new neighbours for you at Villa Bruno, but it is hardly likely that it will be used by another occupant except during the summer months.'

'Ah! will it be let?' asked Francesca, her eyes filling. 'Well, I hope we shall not know the people who take it. For the rest, darling, you can picture me as living the old life, going into Naples on Sunday, teaching Sibyl, rowing with Florestano. But for this next month we are to go for a cruise in the *Pilgrim*, and perhaps next year I may go to England.'

'You would like to be with Clare?'

'Yes; though I suppose father will not like me to tell her now of these three weeks, and it will be hard that she should never know. Carlo, why should not you go to see Clare when you are in England?'

He shook his head.

'She would disapprove too strongly of my change of professions,' he said; 'and it is not a change that I can explain to all the world. Then, too, she lives in your uncle's house, and, after what has happened, he would hardly care to have me there.'

'Uncle George likes you very much,' said Francesca, quickly.

Carlo did not reply, but he thought differently. It was not then, however, that he could care to discuss so trifling a matter; time was passing, and he knew that Captain Britton must already be expecting him to go. The thought broke down all his self-control; his calmness gave place to a passionate outburst of love and grief, which recalled to Francesca his sudden change in the belvedere when he had first asked for her love.

She clung to him now as she had done then, but it was not of love and present bliss which she spoke.

'Patience, Carlo *mio;* patience,' she whispered. 'It is, after all, that which we need.'

The word brought back to him the recollection of his dying father, and calmed the tumult of feeling. He held her sweet face between his hands, looked long into those pure eyes, and grew strong once more.

'*Pazienza!*' he murmured, clasping her again in his arms. 'God have you in His keeping.'

* * * *

At the gate of Casa Bella Mr. George Britton, much to his dismay, chanced to encounter the owner of Villa Bruno, quite the last man he would have chosen to meet. All that he could do was to assume that nothing had happened, and to bid him a courteous farewell, He held out his hand.

Carlo turned upon him a face which haunted the kindly Englishman for many months to come. But, even in his anguish, he could not be otherwise than courteous; a look of effort passed over his deathly features, and,

'With pale lips
That seemed to motion for a smile in vain,'

he said, as he bowed over the Englishman's hand, '*Buon viaggio, signor! A rivederci!*'

CHAPTER XIV.

THE NEW BARITONE.

'Small spheres hold small fires,
But he loved largely, as a man can love
Who, baffled in his love, dares live his life,
Accept the ends which God loves for his own,
And lift a constant aspect.'   E. B. BROWNING.

IT was a hot summer morning, and two ragged little Neapolitans were sauntering along the Chiaja; the elder had flung his arm caressingly round the other's neck, the younger held in his hand a ragged cap full of cherries, from which they were eating contentedly as they walked. A carriage rolled past them, and both boys looked up with sharp, eager eyes.

'*Gran Dio!*' cried one. 'Look! yonder goes Comerio the singer.'

''Tis he himself,' said the other, with a look of interest; 'and in a vile temper, too: his brow is black as a starless night!'

'They say he beats his wife,' said the elder

boy, with a laugh, which was only checked by the offer of a ripe red cherry which his brother held up to his mouth.

Meanwhile the carriage had gone by, and Comerio was, before long, set down at the entrance to Palazzo Forti. He paid the driver, and then, with no very amiable expression, made his way up the long stone staircase and rang the bell.

A maid-servant, whom he had tried unsuccessfully to bribe on former occasions, opened the door to him.

'Is Signor Merlino at the theatre?' he asked, anxious to know whether the coast was clear.

'Yes, signor,' replied the girl. 'What message can I give him?'

'I will give it to Signora Merlino,' said the visitor, preparing to enter.

The maid showed all her teeth in a merry smile.

'But the Signora is still at rehearsal.'

'*Orsù!*' exclaimed Comerio, impatiently, 'I might have known. Well, I will come in then, and wait till they return.'

He was shown into a little ante-room, where for a few minutes he paced to and fro, but suddenly becoming conscious that in the next room someone was monotonously humming *La donna è mobile*, he hastily entered and glanced round. At first nothing was visible, but after a moment or two he discovered the singer, a little brown-eyed boy of four years old, who was perched on the window-sill, and half hidden by the curtain.

'Good-morning, Gigi,' he said pleasantly.

The little fellow flung aside the curtain; he seemed very glad to see the visitor.

'Good-morning, signor,' he said, smiling till his sallow little face looked almost pretty. 'Are there——' he looked longingly, yet hesitatingly, in the direction of Comerio's pocket,—'are there any bonbons?'

Comerio made a gesture of mock despair.

'Why, Gigi, how can I have forgotten? I promised you some *marrons glacés*, did I not? but, indeed, the bad news of this morning drove everything out of my head.'

'What bad news?' said the little boy, with

an anxious look that seemed to be beyond his years.

'I am going away, Gigi; I shall never travel about with you any more. There will be a new baritone,—one who is not likely to carry *marrons glacés* in his pocket, or to play games with you, for he sets up for being a saint.'

'A saint?' said the child. 'What is that? I thought they were things in the sky.'

'A saint is one who is fond of keeping other people in order. San Carlo will spy out in no time what a naughty little monkey you are.'

'I wish he wasn't coming,' said the child, looking ready to cry. 'I don't see why saints want to sing in operas; they should stop in heaven.'

Comerio laughed.

'Quite right, little one, so they should,' he said, patting Gigi's head. 'But look, my Gigi, will you do one little thing for your old friend, to please him for the last time?'

The boy nodded and looked up with bright, intelligent eyes into the wily face of the baritone.

Comerio drew out a letter and placed it in his hands.

'When your mother comes home, run after her into her room, and when you find her alone— quite alone — give this note to her. Do you understand? It is a secret; no one else must know—no one at all.'

'I know, I know; I can keep a secret!' cried Gigi, gleefully. 'Mamma and I often keep secrets from papa, she taught me how, soon as ever I left Salem.'

Comerio gave a cynical smile.

'Mind you do,' he said, commandingly. 'I shall find out if you play me false. And look here, little one, here are two *lire* for you, and you can tell anyone you like that Comerio came to say good-bye to you, and told you to spend that at Caflisch's. There, I must go now. Don't forget me.'

He stooped and kissed the little sallow face, then hastily took his departure, having seen that the letter was securely stowed away in the child's pocket.

Gigi, with a thoughtful look, poked his

closely cropped head out of the window and watched Comerio as he walked down the street. He was hardly out of sight when a carriage drew up at the door,—a carriage with one gentleman seated in it, and with luggage on the box. Gigi's head was promptly withdrawn, and, in a sudden access of terror, he wrapped himself round in the curtain

'I do b'lieve,' he said to himself in English, 'I do b'lieve it is San Carlo.'

After a time he heard the door of the ante-room opened and the servant's voice saying that the Signora would soon be back from rehearsal; then another voice, so clear and sweet that the child almost forgot to be afraid, said in reply, 'Very well, I will come in here, then, and wait.'

The footsteps drew nearer. Gigi shook in his shoes, yet felt a burning curiosity to see the new comer—this dread being who was to be ever on the watch to spy out his faults.

The stranger seemed to walk up to the piano and to turn over the books lying upon it; then there was such complete silence that Gigi felt sure he must be reading, and ventured to peer out from his hiding-place.

He saw that the visitor was leaning in an easy attitude over the piano, his head propped up by his hand, and his eyes bent upon the score of some opera. Gigi could only see his side face, but that fascinated him, and somehow he did not feel any longer afraid. He was impatient to attract the stranger's notice, but, though he moved the curtain, it was of no use, the new-comer seemed quite absorbed in the music he was reading. At last, in despair, Gigi resolved to speak.

'San Carlo!' he said, timidly thrusting his head a little further forward.

The stranger looked up in surprise, and when he saw the quaint little face peeping out from the curtain, he came forward a few steps, looking very much puzzled.

'I don't know,' said Gigi, politely, 'but I think you are the new baritone.'

Something in this address so tickled the stranger that he began to laugh. His laugh was a very pleasant one.

'You have guessed rightly,' he said, 'but I am not so clever, and cannot guess your name at all.'

'I am Gigi,' said the child, gravely. 'Signor Sardoni laughs at my name and says it is only fit for a pony, but then he is only an Englishman and knows no better; though, after all, I like him, and I like to talk in English, as we did at Salem.'

As he spoke, the little fellow lifted a pair of beautiful dark eyes to the stranger's face; his eyes were his only beauty, they were wonderfully expressive, and something in their depths was familiar to the new comer. He came closer and studied the child's face more attentively.

'Gigi,' he said, 'I think you must be my little nephew, though no one has taken the trouble to tell me of your existence.'

'Oh, no,' said the child—they were talking now in English—'I have an uncle, but he is not like you; he is not the new baritone; he is rich, and lives in a beautiful villa in the country.'

'He lives there no longer; the villa is to be

let, and he is coming to live with you,' said the stranger, taking the child on his knee. 'Come, tell me the rest of your name, Gigi.'

'I have three,' said Gigi, with dignity, 'though they alluse call me Gigi for short. My whole name is Luigi Bruno Merlino, and I shall be four next month.'

'Then there is no doubt that I am your uncle,' said Carlo, kissing the child on both cheeks.

But Gigi, with a shrewd look much beyond his years, shook his head emphatically.

'If you are the new baritone, then you are San Carlo, and San Carlo could hardly be my uncle. You set up for being a saint, you know, and are fond of keeping other people in order; and you will never play games, but will alluse know when I do what is wrong. I badly wished you weren't coming, but somehow you are not quite what I thought.'

The child's words were so comical that they carried no sting; Carlo could only smile at them.

'I am glad of that,' he said, patting the

closely-cropped head. 'You must have been expecting a regular ogre.'

'No, not an ogre, but a saint. It was Signor Comerio that told me about you.'

'Ah!' said Carlo, unpleasantly enlightened; 'you see, as Signor Comerio and I have never met, he can only have drawn a fancy picture of me.'

'I am sorry Signor Comerio is going, he was to have given me some *marrons glacés,* but he gave me two *lire* instead just now—at least, he said so. It was a bit of paper, but he said I was to spend it. In America we alluse have proper money. Do you think this paper will really buy me *marrons glacés* at Caflisch's?'

He began to grope in his pocket, and drew forth an envelope. Carlo could not help seeing that it was addressed to Signora Merlino. A sudden recollection flashed across him of his interview in that very room with Sardoni, and of the Englishman's assurance that Merlino watched his wife's correspondence with lynx eyes, and did not scruple to open all her letters. And Comerio had apparently just been to Palazzo Forti.

'How stupid I are!' said Gigi, thrusting the envelope back again. 'Did you see, San Carlo?'

'Yes, I did,' said Carlo, without any comment.

'Signor Comerio said you would always spy out everything,' said the child, pouting. 'It was a secret, and I promised to keep it; and he will be so angry when he finds out.'

'If you promised to give the letter, you must do so,' said Carlo, gravely.

'Yes, but no one else was to see it,' said Gigi, beginning to cry. 'Oh, dear San Carlo, do promise not to tell, for when Signor Comerio is angry he looks so fierce, and it does frighten me.'

'No one shall hurt you,' said Carlo, putting his arm round the child. 'Don't cry, Gigi; I am very fond of you. No one shall hurt you at all.'

'And you won't tell papa?' said Gigi, still sobbing. 'You see there are things that must be kept from papa, and mamma taught me how when I came away from Salem.'

Carlo felt sick at heart; he remembered how on that Sunday a fortnight ago he had first felt the sensation of coming unexpectedly into a network of evil; now he realised that it was in the very midst of this that he had ordained to live, and he shuddered as the little child composedly described his training in deceit.

'Why do you sit looking so silent, San Carlo?—I mean, looking so grave?' said Gigi, drying his eyes. 'Are you angry with me?'

'No, I am not at all angry; but I am very sorry you promised to give that letter and to keep that secret.'

'Are all secrets wrong?'

'No, there are some things we cannot tell to every one, but they must never be things of which we are ashamed. Suppose you had a beautiful diamond, and were travelling along a road where you feared brigands, you would hide your treasure quite away, and that would be right and wise; but, if you had stolen a diamond from a shop in the Toledo, and hid it for fear of having it taken from you, that would be wrong; do you see?'

'And was Signor Comerio ashamed of his secret, and afraid that it would be found out and taken away from him?'

'Yes, he was,' said Carlo; 'and that is why I was sorry you had not said "no" when he asked you to help him.'

'I will say "no" another time,' said Gigi.

'That's right,' said Carlo, kissing him, and then he quickly turned the conversation, afraid that the child might question him further, and lose faith in his mother.

They were still sitting in the window when Anita returned from rehearsal. She gave a little cry of astonishment when she saw her brother, and came forward quickly to greet him.

'Carlino!' she exclaimed, in her excitement returning to his old childish name. 'Are you come already? My husband has only to-day told me of your decision.' She drew him a little away from the child, and the tears rose to her eyes as she said, with more solicitude than she had ever shown for him, 'Dear Carlo, do you realise what you undertake? I know you want to help me—I understood it in a moment—but do you know what this life is? It is no play-work, as some people think; a public singer leads the life of a cart-horse.'

'Plenty of work is what I shall like best,' said Carlo, kissing her. 'If only I can shield you, Nita, I shall be well content.'

She shivered a little, and went on in an undertone,—

'I saw him for a moment at the theatre, after he knew he was to leave the troupe; his face terrifies me to remember, for I know he understands why it is you have taken his place. But Merlino suspects nothing—that is the one great comfort.'

At this moment Gigi trotted up rather shyly.

'Mamma,' he said, pulling at her dress, 'I promised Signor Comerio I would give you this when you were alone, but I forgot, and pulled it out of my pocket just now, and San Carlo saw it; so I may as well give it you now, directly.'

The colour rushed into Nita's face; she made as though she would tear the letter in pieces without opening it, but Carlo checked her.

'Return it just as it is,' he suggested. 'Direct it to him yourself, and I will see that it reaches him safely.'

Nita hastily crossed the room, and enclosed the letter in an envelope; she knew that Comerio would recognise her writing in a moment, and directed it hastily, perhaps hardly considering that by doing so she had crossed the Rubicon.

But Carlo understood, and knew well that only by showing her all possible love and tenderness could he hope to fill this blank in her life.

'You never told me of this little man's existence,' he said, glancing at Gigi, when she had handed him the letter and he had put it away in his pocket. 'You should have brought him with you to Villa Bruno.'

'He had the chicken-pox,' said Nita, indifferently. 'I suppose he took it on board the steamer—indeed, I always thought it a great mistake to bring him away from America, but

Merlino was set upon having him; he is very fond of the child.'

Carlo felt discouraged; it was quite clear that Nita did not even pretend to care much for her little son. She went on in a complaining voice,—

'He was happy enough at Salem, and, indeed, is always begging to go back again. The people there had brought him up, for, of course, I couldn't drag a baby all over the States with me.'

'It was a farmhouse,' put in Gigi, 'and I alluse went out with the pigs every day. I wish there was pigs here.'

Carlo smiled, but thought Gigi deserved better companionship.

'Merlino knew that we should be in America again in another year,' continued Anita, 'but he had some foolish feeling against leaving the child so far off, and so I suppose we shall have to take him about with us for the present. Men don't realise what trouble a child gives. Merlino likes to play with him now and then for ten minutes, but he would never be bothered with him, and he won't let me have a nurse even. It is absurd to expect me to see to him when already I am almost worked to death.'

Carlo thought there was some truth in this, though he was sorry she seemed to have so little motherly feeling; but that her life was very hard he could well believe, and she looked delicate and overwrought.

'How do you manage?' he said. 'Is there no one to help you with him?'

'The stewardess was kind to him when we crossed, and then, when he was ill, the servant saw to him; but really, poor girl, the landlady leads her such a life that she can't spare time to make him look respectable. He hasn't been out since we came to Naples; I couldn't take such a little scarecrow with me.'

'Maria doesn't do anything for me now,' put in Gigi. 'I can dress myself, mamma, quite well, and I haven't been washed at all just lately.'

'You would have been far better with your pigs at Salem,' said Nita, laughing a little, while Carlo, though perhaps not quite so much disgusted as an Englishman would have been, began to revolve schemes for tubbing his small nephew.

'Then you have really made up your mind to stop here as long as we are at Naples?' asked Nita. 'You will find it a contrast to Villa Bruno.'

'Piale will prefer to have me close at hand,' said Carlo. 'And, indeed, I think it will be better every way. Is there a room for me here?'

'Yes, you can have the room where Gigi was ill; there is no need for him to have a room all to himself now that he is well again; he can sleep on the sofa in the ante-room.'

'Oh, don't turn him out,' said Carlo, and the matter ended in a small bed being extemporised for Gigi in a corner, much to his contentment.

'For you know,' he said, trotting after his uncle, 'when it is all dark, I feel so alone; and last night I *really* think there was a cow under my bed.'

Nita retired before long for her siesta, and Carlo, with the assistance of Gigi, took possession of his new quarters, and unpacked his worldly goods. When all was done, he flung himself back in an arm-chair to rest, and Gigi curled himself up like a little dog at his feet. For a time there was silence, then Carlo was struck by a happy idea.

'Gigi,' he said, 'would you like to come and walk with me in the Villa?'

'What's the Villa?' asked the child. 'Do you mean Villa Bruno?'

'No, I meant the Villa Nazionale,—a garden, you know, with beautiful trees. Would you like to come with me?'

'Oh, yes!' cried Gigi, with a beaming face; 'it will be almost like being at Salem again.'

'With the pigs,' put in Carlo, laughingly. 'But look, before I take you we must make you tidy and clean; don't you think?'

'Perhaps,' said Gigi, with a sigh.

'Are there any baths here?'

'Signor Sardoni has one; he is English, you know, and takes it cold every morning,—quite cold; he asked yesterday whether he should lend it to me, but I guess he was only in fun.'

'Run and ask him, with my compliments, if he will really do so,' said Carlo, much amused.

There was an interval in which he dozed a little; presently back came the child, dragging after him an indiarubber travelling-bath, and followed by Maria, whom he had induced to bring a can of hot water, fearful lest San Carlo should expect him to plunge into cold like the English.

Maria, with a broad smile, suggested that he had better have clean clothes as well, and managed to find some for him; she might even have offered to tub him had not the padrona's voice been heard calling her impatiently, and, with a saucy retort to her mistress, she ran off, leaving Carlo and his victim to manage as they could.

Very slowly and reluctantly the tiny fellow divested himself of his clothes, and stood shivering on the brink; Carlo, had he been of an introspective nature, would have been amused at the thought that his first piece of work in his new career was to scrub a grubby little child; being not at all introspective, but extremely practical, he only wondered how in the world he was to do it, and where he was to begin.

'Come, Gigi,' he said, encouragingly, 'I shall pretend you are a pony, as Signor Sardoni says you ought to be; get in quickly and I will groom you.'

Gigi was imaginative, and this notion suited him very well; he began to kick and prance, but no longer objected to the soap and water, indeed, after the first shock he rather liked them; and the scrubbing was at any rate satisfactory work—more promptly visible in its effects than any of Carlo's other work was likely to be. Gigi, who had gone in grim and shivering, came out a beautiful, white, wet, little mortal, with sleek, shining skin, and cheeks glowing like ruddy apples.

'I like it,' he said proudly, 'I like it very much. If I'm good, San Carlo, will you groom me again some day?'

'Every day, till you can do it yourself,' said Carlo promptly, at which Gigi clapped his hands.

'At Salem,' he said, 'we only had Saturday for tub night, and it was so cold in the back-kitchen.'

Carlo, after this remark, thought that whatever the drawbacks of travelling in Merlino's company, the child was better off than in the primitive farm-house with his four-footed friends.

CHAPTER XV.

A DEAR ADVENTURE.

'Next . . . I betook me among those lofty fables and romances which recount in solemn cantos the deeds of knighthood. . . . There I read it in the oath of every knight that he should defend to the expense of his best blood, or of his life, if it so befel him, the honour and chastity of virgin or matron. From whence even then I learnt what a noble virtue chastity ever must be, to the defence of which so many worthies by such a dear adventure of themselves had sworn. . . . Only this my mind gave me, that every free and gentle spirit without that oath ought to be born a knight, nor needed to expect the gilt spur, or the laying of a sword upon his shoulder, to stir him up, both by his counsel and his arm to serve and protect the weakness of any attempted chastity.'

MILTON.

GIGI, much pleased with his appearance, and with the novel feeling of cleanliness, capered away to the *sala* to relate his experiences to Sardoni. Carlo followed him, and found Merlino just awake after his siesta, and looking rather more like a surly bear than usual as he yawned and stretched himself. He roused himself, however, to introduce his brother-in-law to the tenor, not knowing that the two had met before; and they thought it best not to explain, but bowed ceremoniously to each other.

'Papa,' said Gigi, gleefully, 'San Carlo is going to take me to walk in the Villa!'

'San Carlo! what do you mean, child?' said Merlino, his voice softening as he patted his son's head.

'Why *him*,' said Gigi, with an expressive gesture; 'Signor Comerio told me he was San Carlo, and I wondered what saints wanted with operas; but he is oh! ever so much nicer than Comerio said.'

The three men laughed involuntarily.

'Comerio did not at all like getting his *congé*,' said Merlino. 'This is just a little display of spite on his part. When did you see him, child?'

'He came in to say good-bye to me this morning while you were at rehearsal, and he gave me this to spend. Oh, dear, San Carlo, might we go to Caflisch's now?'

'You must not call your uncle by that name,' said Merlino; 'it is rude.'

'Why, I thought it was a kind of politeness,' said Gigi, with a puzzled face; 'and that it was only for the very best things.'

'In that case you had better not uncanonise Signor Donati,' said Sardoni, who had watched the scene with a sort of careless amusement. 'If you'll allow me, Gigi, I will also come with you.'

Carlo looked pleased; he could not have explained why Sardoni attracted him, but already he felt that the Englishman would be his friend. His discovery of Gigi that morning had broken the blank desolateness which for the last four-and-twenty hours had overwhelmed him, and the sight of Sardoni somehow cheered him yet more. Possibly the mere fact that the tenor was Francesca's fellow-countryman prejudiced him in his favour; and then, although the Englishman's careless, witty-looking face was perhaps not of the very highest type, yet there was something winning about it,—something which interested Carlo and took him out of himself and his own cares.

'So you have changed your mind since I saw you the other day,' said Sardoni, as they walked down the Toledo. 'You think stage life may, after all, bear comparison with private life?'

'I am going to try my fortune as a singer,' said Carlo lightly, but revealing in his face all that he strove to banish from his tone. Sardoni drew his own conclusions, but had too much tact to ask any questions.

'I was never more astounded than when Merlino told me the news,' he remarked; 'and I think seldom more pleased: the Company will be well rid of Comerio, who is a double-dyed villain such as one seldom meets.'

'I must own that in looks he gives one the impression of being less of a brute than Merlino himself,' said Carlo, lowering his voice cautiously.

'Looks are not everything,' said Sardoni; 'there are some faces—yours for instance— which can be read in an instant; but there are others which baffle one altogether. Merlino is not so bad as he seems; at any rate while he is a brute the other is a fiend.'

'How did he take his dismissal?' asked Carlo.

'I heard very little about it, but apparently

he has taken good care not to quarrel with Merlino. No doubt he'll move heaven and earth to get into the troupe again, he is not a man who will stand being beaten.'

'Yet Merlino would never have us both, I suppose?'

'No; so it will now be to Comerio's interest to oust you. Don't think me a brute to speak out plainly, but when I caught sight of Comerio's face as he left the theatre I thought I wouldn't be in your shoes for a million of money. That fellow is your enemy, and he may nurse his revenge for years, but, sooner or later, he'll have it.'

A feeling of vague discomfort crept over Carlo; for a minute he was silent, then, with a look on his face which startled Sardoni, he said cheerfully,—

'I owe you a great deal; it was through you that I first knew there was a chance of helping my sister in this way, and now you have taken the trouble to warn me of a danger. One must not dwell on such things, though perhaps it is well to know of them.'

'I should have thought,' said Sardoni, smiling, 'that you would be more likely to curse me than to bless me for having first put into your head a notion that must have cost you dear.'

Carlo gave a quick glance at his companion, wondering whether he had the least conception how great the cost had been. Perhaps he was glad to be spared any direct answer to the remark by their arrival at Caflisch's, and the necessity of helping Gigi to lay out his two *lire* to the best advantage.

Afterwards, they strolled on to the Villa, and, while Gigi played about happily, the two men sat under the trees, Sardoni finding a sort of idle pleasure in studying his new companion.

'Do you mean to sing under your own name?' he asked, after a time.

'Yes,' replied Carlo; 'I have no object in taking a *nom de guerre*; with an English name, of course, it is different—you were almost bound to do so.'

Sardoni gave a sarcastic smile.

'It was most necessary,' he remarked, drily. 'Did my own people know how I gained my livelihood they would be even more ashamed of me than they are already.'

Carlo looked surprised, even a little anxious. His interest in Sardoni grew deeper.

'They do not then know where you are?' he asked. 'That is surely very hard on them.'

The tenor gave a short laugh.

'Not at all; I am silent purely out of regard for their feelings. Do you know what the old Puritans used to call actors? They called them "caterpillars of the Commonwealth" and "vagabonds."'

'That may be, but family feeling must in the end be stronger than such prejudice.'

'You judge others by yourself,' said Sardoni. 'All families are not so devoted as yours seem to be.' Then, his brow contracting sharply, 'Besides, did I not tell you when we first met that, in my own country, men would no longer trust my word as blindly as you seem inclined to do?'

'Why will you always force that upon me?' said Carlo, looking full into his companion's eyes. 'Do you wish to make me doubt you? That is hardly a friendly act, since you are the one light just now in my dark sky.'

The words sounded strangely in Sardoni's ear, the simile was so un-English, but the tone touched him more than he would have cared to own.

'I force this upon you because I like you,' he said, with some effort. 'You are the first man I have seen whose friendship I could have wished. But I will be friends with no man who does not know the truth about me; and whoever knew the truth would not care to be my friend.'

'I should care,' said Carlo, quickly.

The Englishman shook his head. Then, suddenly resuming his usual reckless, nonchalant manner, he said with a laugh, 'Few men, I fancy, have managed to sustain their *nom de guerre* so completely; Merlino himself has not even a notion of my true surname.'

'What induced you to take the name of Sardoni?' asked Carlo.

'Well, according to the character of my questioner I have two replies,' said Sardoni. 'Matter of fact: It occurred to me one morning while I was breakfasting off sardines. Poetic: I assumed it in a sardonic mood, while contemplating a journey to Sardinia. We have some funny improvements on names among us.'

'Are they chiefly Italians in the Company?'

'Oh! we are a very mixed multitude,' said Sardoni. 'I'll prepare you for your future lot and give you a faithful description of the "happy band of pilgrims." Let us be more courteous than the playbills, and take the ladies first. Top of the list stands Madame Merlino, who needs no description. Next comes Mlle. Elise de Caisne, a little French flirt. Then the two mezzos, Mlle. Lauriston, ditto, ditto, and Miss Robinson, who hails from New York, but sings under the name of Duroc: she is an average American girl, and can be pleasant enough, also—which speaks well for her—she is hand in glove with Domenica Borelli. The Borelli is a Maltese lady, in reality Borg— everyone is a Borg in Malta. She is a contralto with a wonderful compass, a real good painstaking artist, the joy of Marioni's heart; there exists between them a platonic friendship. Next we come to the tenors.'

'Headed by Signor Sardoni,' put in Carlo, with a smile.

'And close on my heels,' continued the Englishman, 'follow my two rivals, Crevelli and Caffieri—awfully jealous of me—awfully; not of each other, that's the odd part; but then they are so much alike that it's always a case of " Which is which ?" and when one is praised the other thinks it was a mistake and really meant for him; those two are *bonâ fide* Italians, and as like as two peas,—broad forehead, straight, black hair, correct profile, big moustache, great expanse of cheek. You'll find some trouble in knowing them apart, but at last I've induced Crevelli to keep his hair an inch longer than the other's, just for convenience' sake.

'That brings us to the basses, and to your brother-in-law; we won't discuss him: you'll find that he gets well treated because they all live in mortal terror of him. Then, Gomez. Gomez has raven hair and a sad cast of countenance, he hails from Seville and stands much on his dignity. Tannini, alias Joshua C. Tanner, is a jolly Yankee, and has a keen eye to the main chance. A very practical man is Tanner; he'll soon be "calc'lating that he can't understand such a knight-errant" as you. Next comes Bauer—a good solid lump of humanity, always in at dinner-time and to be found at odd hours tucking in, regardless of the coming opera. He reminds me of an old nursery song of ours, about—

"A duck, who had got such a habit of stuffing,
That all the day long it was panting and puffing."

Bauer's often out of breath on the stage, you'll find. Then there is Donati, the baritone, whose character I have not yet fathomed; and Fasola, a miserable stick, capable only of third-rate parts, but supposed to be your under-study; and, finally, our little conductor, Marioni, who wears himself to fiddlestrings, all out of devotion to the muse, and tears his hair — you'll see presently how ragged it is — because he can't get things done as he would wish.'

'I have heard Piale speak very highly of him,' said Carlo, and then he sat silent for a minute or two, musing over Sardoni's odd description of his future companions, and wondering what this strange new life would be like.

'Was Comerio a favourite?' he asked at length.

'He was hated by some and liked by others; Domenica Borelli, for instance, was not on speaking terms with him.'

'And yet travelled in the same Company?'

'Oh, that is perfectly possible! I don't think she has spoken to him since we were at San Francisco, a year ago, yet of course they had to act together. The Borelli is extremely fastidious, she will highly approve of the change of baritones. But Gomez will hate you, for he is Comerio's friend; I shouldn't be surprised if he got up a cabal against you.'

Again Carlo was silent, he looked down the long, shady walk with its sombre ilex-trees; the prospect of his new life had never before seemed so distasteful to him, and it was with a sense of relief that he caught sight of Enrico Ritter coming towards them with his usual long, imperturbable stride. Enrico seemed his last link with the past, and he was glad to be able to introduce him to Sardoni.

'I have just met your uncle,' said Enrico, abruptly, as he took the vacant place beside Carlo.

'Then, of course, you know all?'

'Yes, and I find it hard to forgive you,' said Enrico.

'To forgive?' echoed Carlo, questioningly.

'Yes, to forgive. You have falsified my pet theory,' said the egoist. 'Here, give me one of your cards and I'll tell you in two words what I think of you.'

Carlo, not without a pang, as he remembered how at first sight of those copper-plate words, 'Avvocato Carlo Poerio Donati,' he had felt himself the happiest man in Naples, handed the card to his friend, and Enrico, crossing out the 'Avvocato,' scribbled above it the words, 'Knight-Errant.'

Sardoni glanced at it with a smile.

'You couldn't have put the case more tersely,' he said, rising to go, because he thought the two friends would rather talk out the matter alone. But before he turned he glanced searchingly at Carlo, and again surprised on his face the look which had perplexed him before.

'Does the fellow actually take pleasure in

giving up his life to the service of that chit?' he thought to himself as he walked away. 'If ever there was a commonplace, uninteresting woman in the world, it is Anita Merlino; she'll not even have the grace to be grateful to him.'

Late in the afternoon of the following day, Carlo, returning from a long lesson with Piale, happened to meet, in the Piazza Municipio, a handsome English sailor whose face seemed familiar to him. He glanced hastily at the name embroidered on his jersey, and read the word *Pilgrim*. With a great hunger in his heart to know Francesca's whereabouts, he turned and accosted the man.

'So the *Pilgrim* is still here,' he said, courteously. 'When does she leave?'

'To-night, sir,' said the sailor, looking pleased at the recognition. 'Captain Britton and the young ladies came on board an hour ago, and we are only waiting now for the caterer; and there he comes yonder.'

Carlo, glancing round, saw another of the yacht's crew, a bluff-looking, elderly man, whose duty was to buy the food for his mates.

'We shall sail now as soon as we get on board, sir,' said the coxswain. 'Can I take any message for you?'

'None, thank you,' said Carlo, and bidding the man a courteous farewell, he turned quickly away. Hurriedly he walked towards the Strada Nuova, and looked across the blue waters of the bay. There was the *Pilgrim*, anchored to the Military Mole, her beautiful white sails all set, and only waiting for the return of the dinghy to raise anchor. Carlo saw the little boat threading its way between the vessels in the harbour, saw it round the yacht and disappear, then descried Oxenberry's lithe figure springing on board. For a few minutes all seemed haste and confusion; he could hear the rattling of chains, and could even make out the figure of the steward seated on the capstan with his concertina, while the sailors heaved up the anchor, swinging merrily round to the familiar strains of the 'Shanty.' Their hearty voices reached him even at that distance, and he remembered how as a child Francesca had proudly taught him to sing the 'Shanty' with a proper English accent.

Fragments of the words seemed now to float across to him, and the tears started to his eyes.

> 'Hurrah, my lads! we're homeward bound,
> We're homeward bound for Plymouth Sound;
> Up with the sail, and off goes she.
> Hurrah, my lads! hurrah! hurrah!'

The cheerful old tune seemed to him now like a dirge,—the dirge for his old life which was passed and over, the dirge for his betrothal so swiftly ended.

All at once his heart began to throb wildly, for he saw a slim, dark figure come on deck with a white shawl wrapped about the head and shoulders. Francesca stood with her face turned towards him, looking to the shore and away from the blithe sailors, whose merry song, perhaps, brought to her mind the very thoughts it had suggested to Carlo. He gazed on, hardly knowing whether the sight comforted or tortured him, but, in any case, unable to move, unable for one instant to relax the strain.

At last the song ceased, the chain rattled no more, the yacht began to move, and Francesca shifted her position a little, but still kept aloof from the rest, still gazed shorewards. And thus she remained while the summer wind filled the white sails, and the *Pilgrim* glided out of the harbour, gently, proudly, but relentlessly, moving out seawards.

To the very last, his eyes rested on her till the slim, black figure became a mere speck in the distance, and finally was lost to sight. He lingered still for the last glimpse of the *Pilgrim's* sails, on which the afternoon sun glinted with dazzling brightness; then, when those, too, had disappeared, he became conscious of a creeping chilliness, which obliged him to grope his way to one of the seats and wait till he had recovered his self-control.

It was a vision of Piale's reproachful face which finally roused him. What would be the Maestro's horror could he see his pupil sitting there regardless of the dangerous hour of sunset, which was fast approaching? He drew himself together and walked slowly back to the Palazzo Forti through the narrow, picturesque streets, so familiar, but now so desolate to him. Never in his life had he felt so hopelessly lonely as when he mounted the dirty stairs and reached the suite of rooms which, for the time being, made his home.

In the ante-room Gigi was crying piteously; in the *sala* Merlino, in one of his worst tempers, was arguing with Anita; while Gomez, who had just arrived from Seville, stood glowering darkly at the new baritono.

END OF THE FIRST VOLUME.